Against The Odds

INTER-TEL

The First 30 Years

In 30 years, Inter-Tel has gone from Steve Mihaylo's one-man shop to a communications pioneer at the forefront of the Digital Revolution.

Against The Odds

INTER-TEL

The First 30 Years

Jeffrey L. Rodengen

Edited by Jon VanZile
Design and layout by Sandy Cruz

*To Lois, Sarah and Emily, for enduring so much for so long,
and to all the wonderful men and women of Inter-Tel
who have given so much love and dedication to Inter-Tel and me.*

— *Steve Mihaylo*

Also by Jeff Rodengen

The Legend of Chris-Craft
*IRON FIST: The Lives
of Carl Kiekhaefer*
*Evinrude-Johnson and
The Legend of OMC*
*Serving The Silent Service:
The Legend of Electric Boat*
The Legend of Dr Pepper/Seven-Up
The Legend of Honeywell
The Legend of Briggs & Stratton
The Legend of Ingersoll-Rand
The MicroAge Way

*The Legend of Stanley:
150 Years of The Stanley Works*
The Legend of Halliburton
The Legend of York International
The Legend of Nucor Corporation
*The Legend of Goodyear:
The First 100 Years*
The Legend of AMP
The Legend of Cessna
The Legend of VF Corporation
The Legend of Rowan

*New Horizons:
The Story of Ashland Inc.*
The Legend of Mercury Marine
The History of American Standard
The Legend of Federal-Mogul
The Legend of Amdahl
The Legend of Pfizer
*Applied Materials:
Pioneering the Information Age*
The Boston Scientific Story
The Legend of Litton Industries

Publisher's Cataloging in Publication

Rodengen, Jeffrey L.
　　Against the odds—Inter-Tel: the first 30 years /Jeffrey L. Rodengen.
　　p. cm.
　　Includes bibliographical references and index.
　　ISBN 0-945903-31-6

　　1. Inter-Tel 2. Computer industry—United States.
　　I. Title

HD9696.C64168 1999　　　　　　　　　338.7'61004'0973
　　　　　　　　　　　　　　　　　　　　QBI97-40428

Write Stuff Enterprises, Inc.
1001 South Andrews Avenue, Second Floor • Fort Lauderdale, FL 33316
1-800-900-Book (1-800-900-2665) • (954) 462-6657

Library of Congress Catalog Card Number 97-60422
ISBN 0-945903-31-6

SECOND EDITION
Completely produced in the United States of America
10 9 8 7 6 5 4 3 2

iv

TABLE OF CONTENTS

FOREWORD

By
Jon Kyl
United States Senator

I'VE KNOWN STEVE MIHAYLO FOR YEARS. I BELIEVE I first met Steve in 1984 through the Phoenix Chamber of Commerce where I was chairman. Two years later, in 1986, I first ran for the House of Representatives, and Steve was very supportive of my candidacy.

Over the last decade, companies like Inter-Tel have just taken off in Arizona. There are many of them — some are start-ups, some were very small that are now respectable middle-sized, and then of course, there are the companies like Intel, Motorola and Honeywell that have really put Arizona on the high-tech map. But Inter-Tel is a unique kind of company. It was among the first in its industry, and it helped create that industry.

As we head into the future, I believe high-tech companies like Inter-Tel will be more of a cornerstone of the economy as we shift away from the Industrial Age kind of structure. This has prompted a very public discussion. There is an intercession of government policy making and this newly evolving economy, leading people to debate questions like taxation and regulation, and modifying laws that were written for the Industrial Age, like antitrust and copyright laws that may need to be modernized to reflect the new high-tech economy. The great debate is how the government interface with this new economy will influence its direction.

There are also concerns about the education of American youth and how we need a better educated citizenry to take advantage of the opportunities provided. When you have to increase immigration caps from other countries where citizens are better equipped to solve problems like the Year 2000 problem, there's obvious concern that the American education system is not doing its job.

This future is going to require a lot more flexibility in our society, and the ability to adjust to change more quickly. This future is going to require great agility, for both corporations and consumers. Companies like Inter-Tel are doing a tremendous amount to help usher in the future. They have gotten directly involved with educational institutions like the universities, understanding that's the best way to meet their needs, and at the same time, provide society with a better standard of living and more educated workers.

The kind of entrepreneurialism required as we head into the next millennium needs visionaries like Steve Mihaylo. He is a thinker. He works very, very hard to implement his original vision. With Steve, I have to say "hard working" because to visit with him, he may seem laid back — but you can always see the drive toward innovation and excellence.

In the end, the ideas he has fostered have created a company, they've helped drive an industry and positioned Inter-Tel right on the leading edge of the Digital Revolution.

Arizona Senator Jon Kyl was first elected to national office in 1986, when he won a seat in the U.S. House of Representatives. In 1994, he was elected to the U.S. Senate, where he became an expert in intelligence and national defense issues. He serves on the Intelligence Committee, the Judiciary Committee and Appropriations Committee.

INTRODUCTION

IMAGINE HOW IT MUST HAVE BEEN SELLING against AT&T 30 years ago. The giant company was one of the largest corporations on Earth with assets greater than General Motors and Exxon combined. It, and the telecommunications system it created, was deemed so important to the United State's best interest that the government had protected the company as a monopoly for decades. By 1969, however, cracks were already appearing in its impenetrable facade, and the courts and government were swinging against it.

As AT&T's position atop its industry crumbled, hundreds of companies were inspired to jump into the equipment market and sell telephone systems against the giant. Called inter-connect companies because their equipment connected to an existing AT&T wire, they ranged from garage shops with a couple of handsets to overseas corporations leaping at the wide-open market.

Among these was a small intercom company called Inter-Tel in Phoenix, Arizona, founded by Steve Mihaylo, who was barely out of college and running his company on little more than sheer determination. Inter-Tel was created around the same time the *Apollo 11* rocket headed for space, and Mihaylo's early days were bursting with that same youthful enthusiasm. But it took more than enthusiasm to sell phones. Customers wanted features. The search for a phone led Mihaylo to Japan, where he agreed to represent a phone that had one unfortunate drawback: Even its own salesmen thought it was ugly, and they quit.

Later, after Mihaylo sold $2 million worth of phones singlehandedly, Inter-Tel went on to develop the inter-connect industry's first small to mid-size business phone system that used a microprocessor. In fact, Inter-Tel even beat out General Motors as the first company to introduce a product using the new Motorola chip in the early 1970s.

Nevertheless, while its technology was impressive, there was no guarantee of success. Companies like Inter-Tel were a dime a dozen, and without significant cash on-hand, it had to run tight just to stay alive. And there were times when it looked like the company wasn't going to make it. During a memorable crisis in the 1980s, Inter-Tel's flagship new phone system turned out to be riddled with bugs. Calls were dropped, whole lines went down and customers were furious.

Yet Inter-Tel survived to prosper, eventually becoming one of the last independent inter-connect companies from its era and moving into entirely new fields of telecommunications as the Internet changed the face of communication forever.

Inter-Tel's formula for success relies on the values that Steve Mihaylo himself has carried into the daily operation of his company, none so fundamental as loyalty. In an industry that regularly eats its young, Inter-Tel has bred a cadre of loyal, long-time employees who have now risen to likely take Inter-Tel past the $1 billion mark in revenue.

Inter-Tel is a disciplined company, yet it is willing to take risks. It is a customer-focused company that even during trying times treated its customers right. It is a high-technology company patient enough to develop products with staying power. It is a doggedly persistent company.

As Inter-Tel passes its 30th birthday and moves into new markets and new technologies, it is fitting to look into the past at the products that were often ahead of their time, at Steve Mihaylo, the founder who imbued Inter-Tel with its core values, and at the many people who worked day and night to build the Inter-Tel enterprise.

ACKNOWLEDGEMENTS

A GREAT NUMBER OF PEOPLE ASSISTED IN THE research, preparation and publication of *Against The Odds — Inter-Tel: The First 30 Years*. The principal archival research was accomplished by my accurate and resourceful research assistant, Kelly Edwards, who was assisted by Kenneth Hartsoe.

The work would also not have been possible without the generous assistance of corporate leadership and people who are close to the company and its executives. First, I'd like to thank Steve Mihaylo, chairman, CEO and founder, who lent us invaluable hours during many interviews and opened his personal photo collection for our use.

Other executives, both past and present, who assisted during the course of the project include: John Abbott, treasurer; Bill Bosse; Terry Buffard in the International Division; Conway Chester; Jim Chumney, senior vice president, engineering; Bob Craft, former boardmember; Craig Dorsey; Karl Eller, former boardmember; Bill Ennist, product engineer, who has been with the company for 20 years and is still with the company; Maurice Esperseth, former vice president of engineering and current boardmember; Jeff Ford, president of Inter-Tel Integrated Systems; John Gardner, general counsel; Mark Hamblin, senior engineer; Gerhardt Klaiber, former vice president of engineering; Kurt Kneip, chief financial officer; Frank Lewis; Perry Logan; Richard Long, former president; Ralph Marsh, former chief financial officer; Ross McAlpine, president of Inter-Tel Leasing, Inter-Tel Solutions and Inter-Tel.net; Ray McCloud, vice president mountain region; Andy Mihaylo; Chuck Mihaylo; John "Happy" Mihaylo;

Matt Mihaylo, who provided many historical photos from his personal collection; Phil Moore, former boardmember; Bill Nicewanger; Chuck Oakley, vice president of operations; Tom Parise, former president; Tom Peiffer, project manager, who generously donated many images and has been with Inter-Tel more than 25 years; Dr. Dave Pheanis, Arizona State University; Craig Rauchle, president of direct sales; Mike Sargent, vice president of marketing; Tina Sargent, assistant to Steve Mihaylo; Steve Sherman, former executive vice president; Norman Stout, president of Inter-Tel Software and Services; Ed Terminy; Barry Wichansky, vice president eastern region;

Judy Pollack at the AT&T Archives was very helpful in supplying photographs from the extensive company archives.

And finally, a very special word of thanks to the dedicated staff at Write Stuff. Proofreaders Bonnie Freeman and Terry Bridgewater, and transcriptionist Mary Aaron worked quickly and efficiently. Indexer Mary Redgate assembled this comprehensive index. Particular gratitude goes to Alex Lieber, executive editor; Melody Maysonet and Jon VanZile, associate editors; Sandy Cruz, senior art director; Jill Apolinario, former art director, and Barry Carmichael, art director; Fred Moll, production manager; Colleen Azcona and Jill Thomas, assistants to the author; Marianne Roberts, office manager; Bonnie Bratton, director of marketing; Rafael Santiago, logistics specialist; and Karine Rodengen, project coordinator.

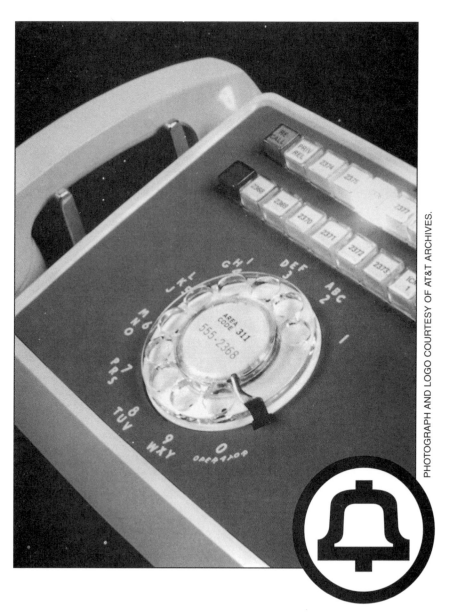

Up until the 1960s and even beyond, the familiar Bell logo was synonymous with phone service and equipment. Competition was a thing of the future.

CHAPTER ☏ ONE

THE DOOR OPENS

"I got here by accident at the second birth of the industry."

— Steve Mihaylo[1]

S TANDING IN THE ATTORNEY'S OFFICE, STEVE
Mihaylo hit a nerve.

Frank Lewis, a partner with Langerman, Begam and Lewis, was listening to Mihaylo's proposal for replacing his phone system — and liked what he heard. It was 1970, and for anybody to be listening to a proposal about buying a phone system from a young guy like Mihaylo was something new. The country was changing rapidly, however. America, not yet plagued by failure in Vietnam or by recession, was celebrating a decade of economic strength.

Only a decade before, a young John F. Kennedy stood before the U.S. Congress and said, "I believe this nation should commit itself to achieving the goal, before this decade is out, of landing a man on the moon and returning him safely to Earth."[2] On July 20, 1969, this seemingly incredible goal was realized and Neil Armstrong captured the world's attention by becoming the first human being to walk on the surface of the moon.

Mihaylo, still in his mid-20s, had founded a small intercom business called Inter-Tel the day after the Apollo 11 carrying Armstrong was launched. "It was electrifying," Mihaylo later remembered. "Back then, it was unbelievable, the conviction and the self-image we had of ourselves in the U.S. That's the backdrop I started Inter-Tel in, that nothing was impossible even though the odds were incredibly long."[3]

The odds in the business phone system sales industry weren't only long, they were stacked against small companies like Inter-Tel. The entire industry had been the exclusive monopoly of AT&T for almost a century. The giant company had invented the phone, built a national network of lines and secured a legal monopoly to control both telephone service and equipment. This monopoly prevented any customer from hooking non-AT&T equipment onto the network, on the basis that it might damage the network and compromise the country's telephone service.

In 1970, however, the situation was beginning to change. A short time before Mihaylo approached Lewis, the Federal Communications Commission handed down the Carterfone decision and paved the way for entrepreneurs to step into a billion-dollar interconnect business.

Like everybody else, Lewis used phones that he had leased from AT&T. The AT&T small business phone system at the time was a standard piece of equipment that had been in place since the early 1960s. Although it was generally a reliable system, there were very few options open to a businessman like Lewis. AT&T had traditionally concentrated its research on the lucrative large-scale central-office systems for the national network instead of on small business systems. So despite the fact that Mihaylo had never sold a pure phone system before, his "I can do it better" pitch found a receptive audience.

"I remember a young guy standing in our reception room saying, 'I'd like to talk to you about your telephone system so you don't have to work with AT&T anymore,'" Lewis recalled in an interview. "Unbeknownst to him, that rang a big bell with me because we had experienced nothing but trouble with AT&T."[4]

Although legally obligated to open its network to other telephone equipment, AT&T was understandably loath to release its profitable stranglehold. Mihaylo explained this to Lewis but also made the critical point that the Japanese phone system he offered was more cost-effective and just as reliable as the system the Phoenix attorney was using.

Lewis was convinced. He agreed to switch over to Mihaylo's phone system and became the first business in Arizona to buy a non-AT&T phone system.

"He explained what he could do, and he was up-front about the fact that we were going to have a lot of trouble with the telephone company because of what he was doing," Lewis said. "They were going to give us a lot of grief because we were hooking up what they then called foreign equipment. They had some euphemism to make you think it was no good. They told you things like you could blow out the whole network. Mihaylo said, 'You know, they're going to fight us tooth and nail.' And they did. I remember the day they were supposed to install it, AT&T was supposed to send somebody down here to switch over the lines and they never showed up. And then the next day, they never showed up and they had all kinds of crazy excuses for not being able to do it. My partners were wondering what the hell I was doing going along with this system."[5]

Mihaylo's phone system was manufactured by Nippon Electric Corporation.

"I wound up buying the system from a company that represented NEC in California. We literally got it in crates. It was a crossbar system that filled a whole wall just to handle maybe 50 or 60 phones. It came like an erector set. You had to wire it together with wire wrap tools, and all of the instructions were in Japanese. I struggled with the system for about a week trying to get it to work, and I kept calling the company in California and saying, 'You've got to get somebody to help me put this system together.' They said, 'Just keep working on it.' Finally I gave up and I sent a telegram to Dr. Kobayashi, the chairman of the board and CEO of Nippon Electric, which even back then was a huge company. Within 48 hours, I had an engineer from Japan in Phoenix. I couldn't believe it."[6]

Beginning a relationship with Japanese technology that lasted until the early 1980s, the engineer helped Mihaylo get his first phone system up and running. "It was a completely mechanical system," Lewis said. "You could hear it clicking and clanging inside the equipment room. But it worked. There was no question about that."[7]

This first sale following "the second birth of the industry" (as Mihaylo would later say, referring to the court decision that made it possible) laid the foundation for the future success of Inter-Tel. Mihaylo quickly sold two additional systems, both to previous intercom customers, and began pushing his little company, Inter-Tel, down a path that would one day take it to the cutting edge of telecommunication technology.

The Carterfone Decision

It's impossible to imagine Inter-Tel, or for that matter modern telecommunications, without a young "tenacious Texan" named Thomas Carter and his long fight with AT&T.

By the 1960s, AT&T was the largest company on Earth, controlling virtually all aspects of telephone service. The company made telephones and monopolized both local and long distance service. Over the previous 70 years, AT&T had built the world's most efficient and most advanced telecommunications network in the United States. It was generally accepted that "Ma Bell" always had been, and always would be, the telephone company. One journalist wrote, "It is perhaps a curiosity of 20th century American life that we no more think of going out and shopping around for telephone equipment than we do of changing family doctors in the midst of a serious illness. You want a telephone? You call the telephone company. It's as simple as that."[8]

As a regulated monopoly, AT&T operated in a competitive vacuum, thus attracting the attention of federal trust busters. The government first brought suit against the giant corporation in 1949 under the Sherman Antitrust Act, but AT&T was left intact. The first real decision against the company came in 1957. It involved a small non-mechanical device called a Hush-A-Phone that slid over the mouthpiece of the receiver to mute background noise so the speaker's voice could be heard. AT&T had prohibited the sale of the piece of "foreign equipment," but the courts disagreed.

By the late 1960s, a new FCC director was ready to take action against AT&T. In the 92 years since its invention, the telephone had reached more than 80 million homes and businesses.[9] But customers encountered a number of problems, and the public was fed up with AT&T. Among other things, customers often couldn't get a dial tone for minutes or even hours; lines went dead in mid-sentence; there were delays in getting telephones installed; and callers were plagued with misconnections, disconnections and malconnections.[10] Throughout 1968, complaints reached the FCC in record numbers.

Enter Thomas Carter. He was president of a small company called Carter Electronics Corporation, which produced a device called the Carterfone. These Carterfones allowed people in remote locations, like oil-rig operators, to communicate with a telephone caller via a two-way radio. When both the radio operator and the caller were in contact with a central base, the telephone handset was simply placed on the Carterfone cradle and a voice circuit automatically switched on the radio transmitter.

Between 1959 and 1966, Carter sold about 3,500 of his devices to dealers and distributors. AT&T, however, hearing about the device, had filed a complaint with the FCC in 1967 proclaiming that the Carterfone was an illegal interconnective device, thus subjecting subscribers to penalties. For legal support, AT&T cited FCC Tariff No. 132, which read: "No equipment apparatus, circuit or device not furnished by the telephone company shall be attached to or connected with the facilities furnished by the telephone company."[11]

Carter brought a private antitrust action against AT&T in federal district court. "It became a whole lawsuit," remembered Conway Chester, a California businessman who co-founded Inter-Tel with Mihaylo and was his partner.

"Carter lost a big cattle ranch and a lot of money and went bankrupt as a result of trying to battle the

telephone company. But it came to pass that other major companies like IBM enjoined behind Carter without actually putting their name out there because they were doing business with AT&T and didn't want to be overt about it. They got behind him because they recognized that if this man didn't prevail, then they would never be able to hook up computers to ship data across phone lines."[12]

In 1968, the FCC took the matter over from the court system and reconsidered its protectionist stance toward AT&T. Citing the Hush-A-Phone decision, the Commission reversed a tariff that had been in place since the Communications Act of 1934.

"There has been no adequate showing that non-harmful interconnection must be prohibited in order to permit the telephone company to carry out its system responsibilities. The risk feared by the examiner has not been demonstrated to be substantial, and no reason presents itself why it should be. No one entity need provide all interconnection equipment for our telephone system any more than a single source is needed to supply the parts for a space probe. We are not holding that the telephone companies may not prevent the use of devices which actually cause harm, or that they may not set up reasonable standards to be met by interconnection devices. These remedies are appropriate; we believe they are also adequate to fully protect the system."[13]

These "reasonable standards" would cause Mihaylo and other interconnection vendors headaches over the years, but the decision had tremendous implications. Telephone customers were free to buy telephone equipment from non-Bell vendors. Mihaylo and thousands of other entrepreneurs like him saw the opportunity of a lifetime as a volatile, multimillion-dollar market opened its doors. The next hurdle, and the one that would ultimately make or break companies, would be to convince customers that a company had the right mix of service and features — and that they were for real.

"When we first started, I'd go out and tell people they could buy their phones from Inter-Tel and they didn't need to go to Bell," Mihaylo recalled. "Several times when I went back for my second appointment, the police would be waiting for me. People just didn't believe it. ... They thought it was some kind of a scam."[14]

AT&T Fights Back

Predictably, AT&T had fiercely resisted the Carterfone decision and quickly became notorious for trying to trample the fledgling interconnect industry. AT&T held the attitude that "foreign" equipment would damage Bell's delicate network and the nation would suddenly be without an operable telephone network. The company's standards for interconnection required a coupling device that was mysteriously hard to locate.

Throughout the late 1960s and 1970s, AT&T was criticized for undercutting the competition when it became a threat and overcharging in areas where competition was absent to compensate for the losses. Stories like the one that appeared in *The New York Times* on August 26, 1969, appeared across the nation: "The New York Telephone Company was charged yesterday with trying to maintain a tight monopoly grip on all phases of the telephone industry by setting below-cost installation rates where there was a threat of competition."[15]

Even though Mihaylo sold equipment, not phone service, he was up against a jealous giant. Sometime after that first installation at Lewis' law firm, AT&T tried instituting a tariff of $5 to $10 per line for the coupling device. Years later, the FCC ruled the practice was discriminatory, and Lewis and hundreds of others were compensated for the charges they had incurred for using non-Bell equipment.

The 1968 Carterfone decision signalled the beginning of the end for AT&T's singular domination in the telecommunications industry. Throughout the years, this development would bring nothing but good news for small businessmen like Steve Mihaylo. But AT&T is not a villain in this story — in less than 100 years, the company effected one of history's most profound changes in human communication.

On March 10, 1876, this liquid telephone invented by Alexander Graham Bell was used to transmit the words, "Mr. Watson, come here; I want you!" after Bell spilled sulfuric acid on himself. They were the first words ever transmitted over a telephone-like apparatus.

THE FIRST BIRTH OF AN INDUSTRY

"I am like a man in a fog who is sure of his latitude and longitude. I know that I am close to the land for which I am bound and when the fog lifts I shall see it right before me."
— Alexander Graham Bell[1]

THE FIRST RECORDED LONG-DISTANCE COM-munication resembled today's highly advanced cel-lular telephones, whose weak signals are passed from cell to cell as the user moves across the countryside.

This first "long-distance call" sped across the French countryside in a series of relays similar to the way a mobile telephone switching station "hands off" cellular signals. The relay device, called a semaphore, was invented in 1794 by a French engineer named Claude Chappe. It gave the French army a way to transmit mes-sages along the 138-mile route from Lille to Paris in two minutes. Chappe's semaphore consisted of a series of towers located on hilltops about 5 to 10 miles apart. Skilled workmen using cranks manipulated wooden sig-naling arms mounted on the towers to represent letters of the alphabet. The messages were read by telescope from a neighboring tower. The French army used 550 such signals.

Chappe's semaphore became known as a "telegraph," which was derived from the Greek words tele, for "distant," and graphein, meaning "to write."

While Chappe's invention might have made military communication possible across France, there was no truly practical way for civilians to send messages over land and no way at all to communicate across water. Communication by newspaper and journal between England and the United States remained crippled by a three-week voyage across the Atlantic.[2] It took 43 years until experimentation with electricity paid off with the first practical electric telegraph.

The first two commercial telegraphs appeared in the same year, one in the United States and one in England. The English telegraph, patented by William Fothergill Cooke and Charles Wheatsone in 1837, used six wires and five needle pointers. A current passing through wires caused the needles to point to specific letters and numbers on a mounting plate. The system found almost immediate use on England's railroads.

Also in 1837, American inventor Samuel F.B. Morse was granted a patent on an electromagnetic telegraph that used a system of dots and dashes to represent letters and numbers. Having received a $30,000 grant from Congress, Morse successfully transmitted the first message in 1843 along 35 miles of telegraph lines between Washington, D.C., and Baltimore. One year later, the system, using wires attached by glass insulators to poles, was opened to the public with the message, "What hath God wrought!"[3]

The business world was quick to respond to the new invention. Scores of start-up telegraph companies quickly strung lines along existing railroad tracks. The first transcontinental line was completed in 1861 by the Western Union Telegraph Company. It connected San Francisco to the East Coast. In 1866, the steam screw and paddle ship Great Eastern laid the first trans-Atlantic cable and connected the budding American telegraph industry to its counterpart in England.

Telegraph communication spread across America rapidly. Within 10 years, Western Union Telegraph Company boasted more than 2,200 offices and 100,000 miles of wire. The telegraph had become so widespread that many coastal towns were incomplete without a "Telegraph Hill" to commemorate the invention's impact on local shipping.[4]

The success and proliferation of telegraphy inspired some to think of future forms of communication. One English newspaper of the period acknowledged that some had already considered a device designed to transmit the human voice. Though advanced in its objective, the newspaper article revealed its contemporaries' lack of knowledge concerning electricity and transmission: "A plate of silver and one of zinc are taken into the mouth, the one above, the other below the tongue. They are then placed in contact with the wire, and words ushering from the mouth so prepared are conveyed by the wire."[5]

Voice on a Wire

Had telegraphs maintained their supremacy, it's possible Morse code might still be taught in conjunction with the alphabet. But in the early 19th century, a French inventor named Charles Bourseul demonstrated that more complex sound could be transmitted electronically by disrupting an electrical contact.

The thread was picked up in 1861 by Johann Philipp Reis, a German who designed an instrument that used a membrane with a metallic strip touching a metal point, which was connected to an electrical circuit. Sound waves caused the membrane to vibrate, thus connecting and disrupting current at the same frequency as the vibration. The current was sent through a wire to a sound box with an iron needle that was surrounded by an electromagnet. As the electromagnet received the fluctuating current, it caused the iron needle to vibrate in exact conformity to the frequency. This vibration was then amplified. The instrument was capable of sending simple tones but could not duplicate the complex wave patterns of human speech, or harmonic telegraphy.

Outside the lab, the public concept of a telephone was largely based on the string "telephones" popular in Europe, which could transmit garbled versions of the human voice. These telephones used a parchment membrane within a cone that was attached by cord to a duplicate unit. Voice vibrations traveled along the cord to the receiving membrane. Children and adults could amuse themselves at distances up to 170 yards.[6]

Thus far, developments in telephony remained confined to obscure laboratories or the playthings of the wealthy. It took a young Scotsman named Alexander Graham Bell to make telephony available to the masses. Born in 1847, Bell was introduced to the study of human speech at an early age. His grandfather lectured about the subject, his mother was hard of hearing, and his father invented the Visible Speech System for educating the deaf. As a young man, Bell was a prolific inventor whose work in airplane and boat design had a significant impact. His true gift, however, lay with speech. By age 21, he had used his father's method to teach a deaf child to speak. Four years later (at the same age Steve Mihaylo was when he founded Inter-Tel), Bell moved to Boston to pursue his budding career. In 1875, he met Thomas Watson, a well-read machinist who would turn Bell's ideas into physical realities.[7]

Bell and Watson rented a small attic for their research and received financial support from two prominent Bostonians: Thomas Sanders, whose child learned to speak from Bell's instruction, and the older Gardiner Hubbard, who invested in the project on the condition that Bell develop a practical harmonic telegraph — a device similar to the one created by the German Johann Philipp Reis several years earlier. Hubbard was adamant on this condition. Although he would later become Bell's father-in-law, Hubbard's fatherly reprimands and stern manner often put off the younger Bell.[8]

By June 1875, Bell and Watson had constructed two devices. Instead of a single membrane transmitting tones to a reed or iron needle, Bell had envisioned a device that had two membranes vibrating in perfect harmony, much like the crude string telephones. He was not, however, attempting to transmit human speech until one day when he clearly heard the sound of a plucked reed from Watson's end as the young assistant made an adjustment. The pair immediately changed course and poured their energy into inventing a system that could transmit complex wave patterns like human voice, much to Hubbard's disappointment. "I have been sorry to see how little interest you seem to take in telegraph matters," Hubbard wrote angrily. "Your whole course ... has been a very great disappointment to me, and a sore trial."[9]

Nevertheless, they tested their first device on June 3, 1875. Although no intelligible speech was heard, the team had managed to transmit something resembling a voice.[10]

"I am like a man in a fog who is sure of his latitude and longitude," wrote Bell on the cusp of his breakthrough. "I know that I am close and when the fog lifts I shall see it right before me." America's centennial year brought high expectations. The New Year's Day edition of *The New York Herald* proclaimed, "The last hundred years have been the most fruitful and most glorious period of equal length in the history of the human race ..." and, rather prophetically, "We are entering a year which will be ever memorable in our annals."[11]

Bell was not alone that year in his efforts to improve communications technology. A Chicago inventor named Elisha Gray, who had co-founded Western Electric Manufacturing Company, was chasing the same goal throughout 1875, but with a slightly different concept. Gray envisioned a device that had matching sets of metallic reeds, each tuned to a different frequency. The reeds could be stimulated to transmit different tones. Although he was able to construct a working prototype of his machine as early as 1874, he couldn't build a transmitter that would send human voices.

Gray and Bell were aware of each other's projects. Concerned with losing the race, Hubbard filed an application on his group's behalf with the U.S. Patent Office on the morning of February 14. A few hours later and half a nation away, Gray filed a caveat for a similar device. A caveat is a declaration of an intent to file a patent on an idea that has yet to be perfected. Since Bell's application was filed several hours earlier (neither inventor had working machines), he was granted patent number 174465 on March 7, 1876, for the electrical transmission of voices. This patent was awarded not only for the working parts of the telephone but for the concept of telephony. It is widely considered to be the most valuable patent ever issued by the U.S. Patent Office.

Three days after receiving the patent, Bell and Watson were conducting another experiment when Watson, listening closely to the receiver cone, heard Bell's voice exclaim, "Mr. Watson, come here, I want you." When Watson rushed into the next room, he was surprised to find that

Bell had spilled battery acid on his clothing. On October 9, 1876, Bell and Watson conducted a successful two-way test over a five-mile cable between Boston and Cambridgeport, Massachusetts. In doing so, they unveiled a working telephone and ushered in a new age of communication.

The telephone's integration into daily life was not immediate. The first commercial installation of the telephone took place in May 1877 at the E.T. Holmes burglar alarm company, but other companies and people resisted the idea that a machine could speak. As telephone historian John Brooks pointed out:

> *"Human speech, as opposed to dot-and-dash code, was considered sacred, a gift of God beyond man's contrivance through science. ... Hearing voices when there was no one there was looked upon as a manifestation of either mystical communion or insanity. Perhaps reacting to this climate, most physicians and electricians took it as an axiom that electricity could not carry the human voice."[12]*

As a result, the public considered "Prof. Bell's Speaking and Singing Telephone" a gimmick and little more than a 25 cent novelty.[13]

A major obstacle to early telephone acceptance was the inability to clearly hear the caller's voice. Amplification was nonexistent in the 1870s. Bell's telephone consisted of a well-designed receiver but a poor transmitter. It was a year before Thomas Edison, hired by Western Union as an in-house inventor, designed an amplifier that consisted of a cavity filled with granules of carbon confined between two electrodes through which a constant current passed. As the current traveled through one of the electrodes, which was connected to a

Above: Thomas Sanders
helped fund Bell's
work. He had invested
$110,000 before his
considerable gamble
paid any return.

Left: Gardiner Greene
Hubbard, a Boston attorney,
became Bell's first business
manager for the telephone
system. He was also
Bell's father-in-law and
a major influence on
the young man's work.

thin metal diaphragm, the granules contracted and expanded and passed their vibrations into the receiver. Edison's transmitter, which would be used in telephones until the 1970s, combined with Bell's receiver to introduce audible voice transmissions — a necessary ingredient for public acceptance.[14]

Now convinced that he had a viable product, Bell, together with investors Gardiner Hubbard and Thomas Sanders, formed the Bell Telephone Company in 1877 and promptly sold it to a group of investors. Despite its youth, the company almost immediately became embroiled in its first patent fight with Western Union. It filed a patent infringement suit in September 1878 against Western Union's telephone operation, the American Speaking Telephone Company. Western Union, itself involved in a battle for control between the Vanderbilt family and Jay Gould, agreed to an out-of-court settlement. The agreement included Western Union's surrender of its telephone manufacturing operation in exchange for Bell's promise to stay out of the telegraph industry. In hindsight, Bell clearly won the upper hand in the agreement.

The Bell Company merged with its newly acquired telephone operation to form the American Bell Telephone Company. In 1881, the company bought Western Electric and established a telephone manufacturing arm. By this time, approximately 100,000 telephones were in service throughout the United States.[15] To connect all those phones, the Bell company established the American Telephone & Telegraph Company (AT&T) in 1885 as its long-distance company.

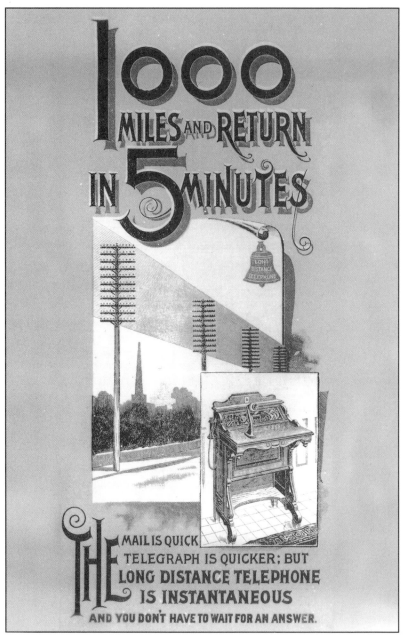

American Telephone & Telegraph, later AT&T, evolved from the original Bell Company. This early AT&T ad pitched the idea of telephony, which seemed unnatural to many people at the time.

CHAPTER THREE

FROM BELL TO BILLIONS

"To make available to all the people of the United States a rapid, efficient nationwide and worldwide ... communication service with adequate facilities at reasonable charges."

— Federal Communications Act, 1934

THROUGHOUT THE LATE 19TH CENTURY, ADVANCing technology brought the phone to within reach of thousands of people. But a truly efficient, plausible telephone network needed a reliable system to route and direct thousands of phone calls. The first manual telephone exchange, with operators patching calls through by hand, became operable in 1878 in New Haven, Connecticut, and serviced 21 customers. Eleven years later, an electromechanical switch invented by Almon B. Strowger was installed in a central exchange that could handle 100 callers. The Strowger switching mechanism was controlled by electric pulses generated by rapidly pushing a button on the transmitter. In 1896, this system was refined into the rotary dial. The first desk sets with separate transmitter and receiver appeared in 1897.

Demand for telephone service grew so rapidly that exchange owners began complaining of too many subscribers as early as 1880. Part of the problem was due to the exchanges themselves. Telephone numbers had yet to be adopted. Even with electrical switches, most large exchanges still used manual switching boards with hundreds of patch cord connections. Subscribers in New York City, with more than 1,500 phones, had to be contacted by name. Telephones were used in hotels, public buildings, government offices and even homes where internal telephone service made it easier to talk to household servants. By 1893, two-thirds of the 260,000 telephones in use were employed by businesses. Businessmen, although accustomed to having a written record of their telegraph transaction, were quickly won over by the telephone's ability to immediately convey information.

As uses for telephones grew, an infrastructure sprung up to service the industry. Single-strand iron wire using a ground wire was replaced by more efficient pairs of copper wire. Common system batteries were replaced with wet batteries, which often leaked, and underground cable eliminated interference caused by new electric and streetcar power lines. When Bell's original patents expired in 1893 and 1894, dramatically reduced prices caused subscriptions to skyrocket and new opportunities to develop.[1]

The battle for control over the lines developed immediately. Independent (non-Bell) telephone equipment manufacturers, such as the Monarch Telephone Manufacturing Company and the American Electric Telephone Company, found ready markets for their products. Meanwhile, the American Bell Telephone Company's manufacturing operation, Western Electric, adopted a policy of refusing to sell telephone equipment to independents. Its parent company, American Bell, with an established network of lines and long-distance service, began to refuse interconnection to independent companies. American Bell and its competitors were accused of using bribery, burglary, spying, sabotage and political maneuvering against each other in the fight to win customers. When a competing exchange in San Francisco had to close its doors and competition in the market was eliminated, American Bell simply raised its charges to customers by $40 to $60 per year.

Although Bell could claim earnings of $5 million by the end of the decade, independent companies had made considerable progress in the West and Midwest. In Michigan, for example, telephones serviced by independent companies outnumbered American Bell telephones by 2,000. Financial returns for the year 1900 showed American Bell with 800,000 telephones and more than $120 million in assets, while independent companies operated more than 600,000 telephones with assets of $55 million.[2] As a reflection of how important long-distance service had become, AT&T became the parent company of the Bell system in 1899.

The early 1900s ushered in a new zenith of competition between AT&T and the 3,000 or so independent companies. The independents were traditionally established by mutual subscribers and shareholders who desired telephone service in their area. They used every means at their disposal, and service could be quite crude, such as using a barbed wire fence for transmission wire in one rural area. By claiming to be the only link to rural communities and portraying themselves as fighting a "foreign competitor," independent companies were able to claim fully half of the market by 1907.[3]

Aware of this threat, AT&T fought back with business muscle, assets and political clout in a manner later referred to by the Federal Communications Commission as "slow financial strangulation." In Buffalo, New York, for example, an independent franchise was guaranteed an operating grant on the condition the company provide 100 telephones with service free of charge, a 3 percent receipt tax on the company's gross revenue, and an up-front cash payment of $50,000. Under such conditions, many independent telephone companies went bankrupt. AT&T's fight to maintain market share, however, produced alarming debt.[4]

Between 1902 to 1907, the company's debt soared from $60 million to $200 million, while independent companies continued to make inroads into the phone business.[5] To bring stability, AT&T brought in Theodore N. Vail, who had been general manager from 1878 to 1887. Vail was an aggressive businessman who sought to achieve a monopoly for the young American telephone system — a goal he spent the next 12 years achieving. He favored, and partially pursued, a policy of vertical integration in which the company designed and manufactured its own equipment, thus guaranteeing quality and cost control. Organizationally, he consolidated the Bell operating companies into regional and state units and acquired many of the smaller independent operations. Bell's oldest competitor, Western Union, was acquired in 1910.

Financial backers saw the possibility for short-term profit, and AT&T attracted some of the nation's most powerful people. By 1907, banking tycoon J.P. Morgan's financiers replaced the original Boston investors and demanded an immediate reduction in expenses. One thousand two hundred jobs were cut. Vail's vision of "one policy, one system, universal service" helped give AT&T new direction and long-term planning.[6] In fact, the structure Vail imposed on AT&T would prove so resilient it lasted until a federal trust-busting suit in 1984 broke the company's grip on telecommunications.

Service Improves

Throughout these years, telephone technology continued its steady forward march. The phone was quickly becoming a necessity rather than a luxury. The original single, uninsulated wire had been completely replaced by hard-drawn copper wires that ran in pairs. Copper wires eliminated such problems as high attenuation and radiation loss, but it was quickly discovered that amplification was going to be a problem. Also, as the distances stretched out farther and farther, cross-talk between the many wires became a significant nuisance.

These problems were attacked from various directions. Loading coils placed at regular intervals along the line significantly reduced distortion and quickly caught on. The development in 1905 of the Shreeve Repeater, a microphone mechanically attached to the receiver that dramatically improved voice amplification during conversation, expanded long-distance service between Chicago and New York.[7] In 1907, Lee De Forest patented the vacuum tube, a powerful amplifier that made transcontinental telephone communication possible. The first transcontinental telephone line, between New York and San Francisco, was established in 1915.

Widespread public acceptance of the telephone was aided by publicity campaigns that portrayed the telephone being used in all walks of life. AT&T had play-by-play reports of the annual "big game" between football rivals UCLA and Stanford phoned into Palo Alto. Stanford's president later used the telephone to address an alumni gathering in New York City. Prominent citizens, such as newspaper magnate Randolph Hearst, were seen using the telephone in movie theater newsreels. Novelist Marcel Proust even wondered in his masterpiece *Remembrance of Things Past*, " ... how it was that none of our modern Bouchers or

Fragonards had yet painted instead of 'The Letter' or 'The Harpsichord,' this scene which might be entitled 'At the Telephone.'"[8]

The rapid spread of telephones was threatened during the years immediately prior to World War I, when government regulation became a real possibility. In 1913, the Department of Justice began looking into possible violations of the Sherman Antitrust Act by AT&T, which still refused to allow interconnection of its lines.

AT&T's acquisition of Western Union three years earlier also raised eyebrows among government investigators. In a letter to the United States attorney general, AT&T Vice President Nathan Kingsbury suggested that in the future, AT&T would no longer purchase independent telephone companies without government approval, and the remaining independent companies would be allowed to interconnect to AT&T lines. This compromise, known as the "Kingsbury Commitment," ended the immediate threat of government regulation.

When the United States entered World War I, however, the federal government regulated the telephone and telegraph industries. The government raised prices, established installation charges and helped unify the industry. Since AT&T was the only company with enough resources to buy independent companies and consolidation was necessary to help spread the telephone, the Justice Department agreed to amend the Kingsbury Commitment. The Willis-Graham Act of 1921 allowed the Interstate Communications Commission to waive antitrust limitations regarding the purchase of telephone companies.[9]

As the Roaring '20s arrived, the telephone company worried less about government regulation and more about automobiles. In 1920, 26 percent of American families owned an automobile, up from only 1 percent 10 years earlier. The successful incorporation of electronics into daily life during the twenties caused Americans to spend excess cash on radios and automobiles instead of telephone service. Residential telephones comprised only 35 percent of subscriptions in 1920. With the help of well-placed advertising campaigns linking telephones to sociability, that figure rose to 42 percent, with more than 15 out of every 100 people owning a telephone. Widespread installations of pay phones also encouraged residential subscriptions. More than 300,000 such phones were installed during the decade.[10]

In 1925, AT&T Chief Executive Officer Walter Gifford combined the research and development operations of AT&T with those of Western Electric to form Bell Telephone Laboratories. This new research powerhouse began producing improvements almost immediately. Carrier transmission systems expanded long-distance service by enabling a caller's voice to be carried at a higher frequency than before, increasing the number of conversations able to be carried by a single line. Ship-to-shore and air-to-ground telephone communications were introduced. Radio programming became widespread.

The earliest "fax" machines even came into use. The concept of sending a picture over a wire had been successfully demonstrated in 1902 by a German named Arthur Korn. His device used a selenium photocell to sense an image wrapped on a transparent glass cylinder. The receiver translated the image onto photographic film. By 1924, AT&T was ready to introduce an improved facsimile system that was used to send pictures from political conventions in the Midwest to newspapers in New York City. These facsimile machines used matching transparent cylindrical drums whose rotation was matched between the transmitter and the receiver. A positive transparent image was scanned by a vacuum-tube photoelectric cell, and the signal was sent over the telephone line. At the receiver, a negative was exposed by a focused beam of light whose intensity was governed by the output of the photo-electric cell in the transmitter. This system could send a five-by-seven-inch photograph in seven minutes with a resolution of 100 lines per inch.

Commercial trans-Atlantic telephone service was established in 1927, and even the U.S. president could finally boast of having a telephone on his desk in the Oval Office. Prior to the Hoover administration, presidents used an enclosed booth outside the executive office. With more than 20 million telephone installations in service by 1930, the industry appeared to be in a permanent growth curve, but as America entered the Great Depression, the landscape changed once again.[11]

During the first three years of the decade, 2.5 million residential subscribers disconnected their telephone service — a loss of 20 percent. Business subscriptions declined 11 percent as did auto registrations and electric service. Financial hardship wrought, in part, by an economic system relatively free of government intervention encouraged the concerned American public to welcome Franklin Delano Roosevelt's approach to solving the country's problems. Unemployment and government indifference towards business practices were replaced by New Deal work programs and regulation. The Federal Communications Act of 1934 sought "to make available to all the people of the United States a rapid, efficient nationwide and worldwide ... communication service with adequate facilities at reasonable charges."

The Act combined the Interstate Commerce Commission, which had focused on trucking, railroad and bus issues since before World War I, with the Federal Radio Commission, a 7-year-old regulatory agency that policed the chaotic frequencies of the infant radio industry. The new Federal Communications Commission was given the task of approving construction and consolidation, overseeing rates, and investigating industry practices. From then on, FCC rulings would play a major role in establishing telecommunication practices.[12]

As telephone executives scrambled to adjust to the new playing field, improvements in telephony continued. An experiment using coaxial cable, a new type of cable composed of two enclosed transmission wires, demonstrated that several hundred two-way conversations could be supported by a single line. This discovery led to phenomenal increases in long-distance use and efficiency.

Perhaps the greatest advances took place in switching technology, which was crucial to expanding telephone service. The first AT&T No. 1 crossbar system was installed in Brooklyn in 1938. The mechanical crossbar switching system had been invented in 1913 by J.N. Reynolds, an engineer with Western Electric. The crossbar was a mechanical grid of five horizontal selecting bars and 20 vertical hold bars. Input lines connected to the hold bars and output lines connected to the selecting bars. The five selecting bars could be moved upward or downward to make connections, thus making it possible for up to 10 simultaneous connections to be made with every switch.

By the time President Roosevelt delivered his second inaugural address in January 1937, the telephone industry was again growing at an annual rate of 6.25 percent.[13] AT&T controlled 83 percent of U.S. telephones and 98 percent of all long-distance telephone lines. In addition, the company manufactured 90 percent of all U.S. phone equipment.

When World War II broke out, the growing civilian phone industry was hampered by government demands on America's communications infrastructure. Conversely, research for the military and heavy investment to increase transmission capacity in the established telephone infrastructure provided new technologies. Digital transmission, a technique that converted analog voice signals into digital bit streams, capitalized on coaxial cable technology. The United States Army Signal Corps' success at bouncing radio signals off the moon proved that long-distance communication with relatively low power requirements was possible. Microwave radio relay and the transistor, which replaced cumbersome vacuum tubes, introduced solid-state electronics and put the electronic switch within reach.

By the end of the decade, demands for telephone service had increased nearly as much as during the first four decades combined. With these demands, however, came new ideas and new products, and when these devices began tapping into telephone company networks, the hearings calendar at the FCC began to fill up.[14]

AT&T Fights to Keep Its Monopoly

AT&T could refuse service to anyone tapping into its lines with "foreign" equipment, i.e., any telephone device not supplied by the telephone company. The company's argument was based on the notion that such equipment would damage its network. From 1937 to 1945, telephone equipment manufacturers Dictaphone and SoundScriber sold more than 15,000 telephone recorders to customers who connected the device to network lines to record telephone conversations. Bell, having received 41 orders to install such devices in 1945, frowned upon the device. The FCC stepped in by 1947 and established technical standards and rules regarding telephone recorders. Although the decision was a disappointment to private users of the devices, it was the first government ruling that allowed foreign equipment to be connected to network lines.[15]

The Justice Department, meanwhile, was in the midst of preparing an antitrust case against AT&T. The case, which was filed in 1949, claimed that since AT&T's Bell operating companies purchased all of their telephone equipment from Western Electric, AT&T held a "captive monopoly." The Justice Department sought to divorce Western Electric from AT&T.

Rather than lose its powerful manufacturing arm, AT&T agreed in 1956 to restrict monopolistic practices and maintain its patent licensing provisions to ensure competitive manufacturing. The consent decree settlement did little to change AT&T's operations except for keeping it from computer-related markets, an area AT&T expected little from. The consent decree also secured some market share for independent telephone equipment suppliers but reserved most of the market for AT&T.

In November 1956, the same year AT&T agreed to its token settlement to stay out of the computer industry, the promising interconnect industry received a boost from another direction.[16] In arguably the most important development of the 1950s, the FCC began investigating a case filed in 1948 by a businessman named Harry Tuttle. The entrepreneur had invented the Hush-A-Phone, a small, $10 plastic cup-shaped device that slipped over the mouthpiece of a telephone. It was popular with speakers desiring privacy or in offices needing to diminish background noise. Tuttle had sold 125,000 Hush-A-Phone units since its invention in 1921 but had become frustrated with retail outlets refusing to carry the product due to its possible violation of the AT&T tariff ban on foreign equipment. He filed a complaint with the FCC, and after several years of investigation, the Commission ruled against the Hush-A-Phone, supporting AT&T's argument that the plastic device usurped the telephone company's authority by reducing transmission quality.

"The significant factor here is the Hush-A-Phone's feature of providing privacy to a talker in a quiet environment," the ruling stated. "This benefit, however, does not balance the public detriment involved in the loss which ... is caused in intelligibility, together with other adverse effects which ... result from the use of the Hush-A-Phone."[17]

Tuttle appealed, claiming the FCC was negligent for not informing AT&T it was "unlawfully interfering with the natural and inherent rights of a subscriber to use an office device related to the efficient conduct of his business." In an unprecedented decision, the three-judge panel of the appeals court ruled in Tuttle's favor, claiming the FCC had indeed exceeded its authority.

The appeals court condemned the foreign equipment provision as an " ... unwarranted interference with the telephone subscriber's right to use his telephone in ways which are privately beneficial without being publicly detrimental." The panel went on to criticize AT&T's suggestion that a caller simply cup his hands to get the Hush-A-Phone effect: "To say that a telephone subscriber may produce the result in question by cupping his hand and speaking into it but may not do so by using a device which leaves his hand free to write or do whatever he wishes is neither just nor reasonable." At Tuttle's insistence, the foreign attachment rule was revised. From now on, subscribers could connect foreign equipment as long as it did not harm telephone company employees, property or service.[18]

AT&T's single-handed dominance in all aspects of the telephone industry was nearing its end, beginning with the equipment portion of its business. While this would be a boon to both consumers and thousands of small-business men and women, the company's extraordinary contribution to technology is almost unrivaled in history. Throughout the early 1960s, for instance, the predecessors to many modern technologies were introduced. The first electronic switching system (ESS) debuted in 1960. Known as the No. 1 ESS, this AT&T system could serve as many as 65,000 two-way voice circuits. In 1962, the Bell 103 modem became commercially available, using technology that had been developed for the Defense Department in the 1950s. This first modem could transmit data at 300 bits per second over conventional telephone lines. The first experimental videophone, known as the Picturephone, was developed in 1963 by Bell engineers. The same year, AT&T began offering Touch-Tone dialing, which was twice as efficient as the rotary method.

Driven by these new technologies and ever-increasing demand for phone service, AT&T continued to grow rapidly. By the 1970s, it was the world's largest company, with more assets than General Motors, the Mobil Corporation and Exxon combined. But with the seemingly insignificant Hush-A-Phone decision, the ball was beginning to unravel. In 1968, a new FCC director named Bernie Strassburg came into office determined to open the doors for small companies like the one headed by the tenacious Texan named Thomas Carter. With the historic Carterfone decision, the floodgates to the interconnection equipment business opened, and a young, ambitious Steve Mihaylo found himself in a Phoenix attorney's office successfully selling against Ma Bell.

Steve Mihaylo joined the Army in 1961 at the age of 17. He received his technical training in the military.

CHAPTER FOUR

STEVE MIHAYLO

"One should love his work so much that he looks forward to each new day with eagerness. Work that is interesting and fulfilling is not work; it is recreation and refreshment."

— Anne DeRitis[1]

STEVEN GEORGE MIHAYLO WAS BORN NOVEMBER 12, 1943, in Los Angeles, California. He was the second of John and Antoinette "Anne" Mihaylo's five sons.

Before she was married, Anne had traveled to Hollywood from Rochester, New York, in the middle of the Great Depression. She made the 2,600-mile trek with her brother Vincent DeRitis in a sleek, open-cockpit two-seater car he had built from spare parts. "When we had saved $250, we started out for California. Our trip lasted 19 days. We drove in a little open car, pulling a trailer, which contained all our worldly goods. We were both really carefree and contented for the first time in our lives," she wrote in a 1960 autobiography.[2]

Anne and Vincent traveled by day and camped in roadside fields at night. They took their time, stopping at

Niagara Falls and spending a week at the Chicago World's Fair. For Anne, who had suffered through an unhappy childhood in Rochester, the trip to California represented a chance at a new life. "We gloried in every minute of it," she remembered.[3]

Before graduating from high school, Anne was forced by her father to attend the Rochester Business Institute and receive secretarial training. After she graduated from the program, she began a "half-hearted business career," although her true ambition — one she had held since she was eight years old — was to become a nurse. "I had a burning desire to take care of and to help other unfortunate people," she wrote. "I happily started on the academic course in high school, thinking it was to be fulfillment at last. But this was not to be. When I told my father I wanted to be a nurse, he flew into a rage and said nursing was no fit profession for a girl."[4]

Once in Los Angeles, Anne and Vincent settled into a house and wrote long, happy letters to the family back home. "We had written too enthusiastically," she said. One by one, the DeRitis family began to move out to California and crowd the little house. When money became tight, Anne quit her office job and went into domestic service so she could live away from home and save money.

In 1936, two years after arriving in Los Angeles, Anne took a bus trip back East to visit her family. Her seat partner was a young Marine named John Mihaylo, and the two "talked constantly for three days."[5] John had run away from home at age 16 to join the Marines and was still enlisted when he met Anne 10 years later. From the moment they boarded the same bus in Salt Lake City, John set his sights on the young Anne DeRitis and pursued her energetically. Four months after they met, John proposed to her and she accepted. The marriage was set for the following June.

In the meantime, Anne moved back to Los Angeles and landed a job as a personal secretary for a "very wealthy woman." A fantastic cook, Anne found herself catering events for some of Hollywood's elite, including Edward Robinson, Howard Hughes and director John Gulding. "I can just envision her in the kitchen, standing by the door trying to hear what they were saying," Steve remarked.[6] Throughout, she received ardent love letters from John.

At the appointed time, Anne traveled back to New York to get married. "As I look back, I don't know how he persuaded me to marry him," she remembered. "I must have been mesmerized by his devotion and attention."[7] The early years of their marriage were like an extended honeymoon. The couple moved from New Jersey to Los Angeles, and then John was transferred to a 14-month stint in Guam.

When he returned, Anne and John established a permanent home in Los Angeles and had the first of their five sons: John, called "Happy," was followed by Steve, Chuck, Matthew and Andy. Anne had consciously tried not to marry a man like her father, but as she watched her boys grow up, she realized that John Mihaylo had the same disciplinary streak she had fled from as a young girl.

She couldn't, however, leave her husband. She had five young boys to care for, and money was always an issue. "I remember her always saying 'mama mia,' which means 'my mother.' Whenever she got mad at us, that's what she'd say. And she'd say, 'My mother would be going insane if she had to deal with all of you,' or something like that. Five boys were a handful," Steve said.[8]

In 1950, the Mihaylo family moved to the Los Angeles suburb of Arcadia. The rural community gave 8-year-old Steve plenty of room to roam. The single-acre property had chickens and other animals. Although money was tight, Anne had taken an interest in nutrition while pregnant with

Steve, and the house was always filled with the smell of baking breads. Steve's younger brother Matthew recalled, "She used to buy flour in these big barrels, and she always made bread. The kitchen was the center of our house, and it seemed like Mom was always in there cooking. She made everything. We hardly had any store-bought food."[9]

With her interest in nutrition, Anne befriended renowned nutritionist and author Adelle Davis when she was pregnant with Steve. The two became lifelong friends, and in her book, *Let's Have Healthy Children*, Davis wrote, "A mother who was applying good nutrition to her five young sons cornered me after church. 'Miracle of miracles!' she exclaimed. 'The kids have stopped fighting. They even can talk in moderate voices. Our house has been bedlam for years, but now I think maybe I'll survive.'"[10]

Davis was writing about Anne Mihaylo.

Hard Times Get Harder

In 1952, however, things took an unpleasant turn. After 15 years of marriage, Anne finally filed for divorce. By this time, John was no longer in the Marines but worked as a Los Angeles County sheriff's deputy. "My fear was very great, but my frustration and anxiety for the welfare of my children was greater," Anne wrote.[11]

Although Anne won custody of her sons, the task of feeding and clothing five growing boys was overwhelming, and John's meager financial support covered only one-third of their living expenses. Later in life, Steve would blame his father for the events that ensued. "He was a bitter individual. He was always blaming my mother for the divorce. I think his idea of how you got back at somebody was to take her kids from her. So he used the economic angle. He didn't give her that much in child support, and she really couldn't afford to take care of us."[12]

Immediately after the split, Steve's older brother, Happy, ran away and left Steve as the eldest sibling. Later referring to Steve as "the real head of the family," Happy said he ran away because he received the brunt of his father's harsh nature and wasn't ready to take on the responsibility of taking care of his younger brothers.[13]

John Mihaylo remarried three years later but took an early retirement after he was badly beaten in the course of serving an arrest warrant. According to Andy Mihaylo, the early retirement was "really his downfall. He became very sedentary and didn't do a whole lot. He ended up moving out to the desert in Palm Springs and living in a trailer in a kind of hermit's lifestyle."[14]

Once on her own, Anne again took a job as a domestic worker. Although it was a difficult time, she was finally free to pursue her life-long ambition. Three years after securing her divorce, she enrolled in the Vocational Nurse Training Program at Pasadena City College and graduated as a delivery room nurse. Anne also became a born-again Christian and "put her trust in God."[15]

But Anne couldn't stretch her small income far enough to meet her large family's needs. When it became clear that she couldn't support the family, Steve and his three younger brothers, Chuck, Matthew and Andy, were sent by their father to live with "Auntie Knappen" in a foster home off Sunset Boulevard in Hollywood. It was the first in a series of foster homes.

From a child's perspective Auntie Knappen resembled Mrs. Mann in *Oliver Twist*: a woman who crowded children into her home and skimped on food and medical services so she could increase her profits. "I think she made her profit by starving us," Steve recalled. While the Mihaylo brothers were there, Andy Mihaylo recalled, at least four or five other children were also in residence.

The children were forbidden to speak at the dinner table and were punished for trespasses with the smack of a wooden spoon on the back of the hand. More severe crimes, such as talking back, were punished by banishment to the narrow stairway in the hall from sunrise to sunset without food. Andy, Steve's youngest brother, was three years old and fared the worst. Within the year he fell ill, afflicted with what was thought to be scurvy.[16]

As Steve watched his younger brothers struggle to survive and his older brother gone, he assumed more and more responsibility.

> *"We'd never been away from our parents or anything like that, and these people were pretty cold and impersonal. It seemed like we never got enough to eat. It took me about four or five months, I think, to get the courage to ask them for second helpings, and to my surprise, I got second helpings. Within a few weeks after that, we were all getting second helpings."*[17]

In those turbulent times, Steve and his brothers were drawn closer in an all-for-one, one-for-all mentality. Andy recalled, "Steve was always very protective. And we were all very protective of the fact that we were brothers and that we had to stick together even in the midst of some difficult living circumstances."[18]

Sundays at Auntie Knappen's offered the four young boys a respite from the uncertainty of their situation. On Sundays, Anne would arrive to take the kids to church and then to a park or to her sister Julie's in El Segundo. At Julie's, Steve was surrounded by some sense of normalcy as his mother and his aunts cooked Italian food in the kitchen and his uncles played cards in the dining room.[19]

Like his mother, Steve was industrious and determined. As Anne worked towards getting an education and her children back, Steve landed his first job as a paper boy for the *Los Angeles Herald Examiner* and helped to offset his and his brothers' living expenses. Unlike the other paper boys, who delivered 30 to 40 papers on their bicycles, Steve delivered more than 300.

With his first job, Steve's penchant for selling took root. He later recounted how he set the record for subscription sales.

> *"I remember my route manager saying, 'We're going to have a contest to see who can sell the most subscriptions in one day.' He said, 'the previous record was 50 subscriptions.' I said, 'I'm going to beat that record.'*
>
> *"I started banging on doors about 6 a.m. Saturday morning and got my 51st subscription at 11:59 p.m. that night. The following Monday I turned them into my manager, and he just went bonkers. He said, 'I was just kidding, the last record was 20,' and I had gotten 51."*[20]

In the years between 1953 and 1957, Steve and his brothers lived in two different homes, and they were headed for another. For the next two years, they would live with the Chrisman family in Big Bear Lake, California. Although it was yet another foster home, the Chrisman family offered Steve the stability and discipline he had been lacking since his parents' divorce.

Back with Anne

The Chrisman house was situated in a large wooded lot next to Big Bear Lake, and whenever Steve found idle time, he took a fishing pole down to the lake to catch trout. But free time was not easy to come by. During the summer months, Steve and his brothers were busy painting the house, doing yard work or chopping the 75 to 100 cords of wood needed to heat the house during the winter. Likewise, winters were spent shoveling snow or hauling wood into the house.

Perhaps the biggest impact the Chrismans had on Steve was to nurture a strong work ethic. Mr. Chrisman was an aerospace engineer who was home only on the weekends. "He was a good stable figure in my life, so those were good years, but he worked us like slaves," Mihaylo said.[21]

By 1959, however, Anne was able to take her four youngest boys back. Although she enjoyed her work as a delivery room nurse, she had re-enrolled in school, earned her high school diploma and was on her way to becoming a registered nurse. For Anne, graduating as a registered nurse represented the culmination of a lifetime's ambition and hard work.

The same year his four younger brothers moved back home, John "Happy" Mihaylo returned to California. Since leaving home, Happy had been traveling throughout the Americas and the Caribbean working as a yacht crew member. He learned to fly at the age of 14 while stuck in Nicaragua and frequently visited the United States. In 1956, he was forced by his father to join the Marines. By 1959, he had settled somewhat, and Steve even moved in with Happy, his wife and baby boy for a short while.

Throughout the years of moving around, the four younger boys forged a very tight bond that Steve later carried into his business relationships. Youngest brother Andy remembered an incident that illustrated the lasting loyalty among the Mihaylo clan.

"One summer right after school let out, my brothers all decided that we would get mohawks. Steve was the

one working the clippers, and me being the youngest, I was the first to do it. But the clippers slipped and they went right across the top of my head. The mohawk was out. We decided to get Yul Brynners instead, and there I was with a totally shaved head. And all the rest of the three of my brothers, including Steve, submitted to having that done. I always kind of marveled at that as I got older that they didn't just give little brother a Yul Brynner and make fun of me."[22]

Enlisted

The brothers didn't remain together for long after moving back in with their mother in 1959. Unable to get her boys under control, she sent them different ways again. Steve went back to live with the Chrisman family. His brothers Chuck and Matthew were sent to live with a local pastor and his wife in Monrovia, California, while Andy remained with their mother.

Unfortunately, the Chrismans could not keep Steve out of trouble either, and he soon wrecked a friend's truck. He spent a year painting cabins to pay for the damage he had caused. Then in 1961, a few weeks after his 17th birthday, his father, infuriated by the truck incident, forced Steve to joined the Army before receiving his high school diploma. He was the second Mihaylo brother to join the armed services under duress.

Faced with the decision of serving four years in the Marines, Air Force, or Navy, or three years in the Army, he chose the shortest route out of the service. "It was my dad that marched me down to the recruiters and probably held my arm up while I said 'I do' or whatever the oath was," he remembered.[23]

The discipline of the Army, and a twist of fate, snapped Steve out of his rebellious phase and set him on a new course. He was sent for basic training to Fort Ord in Monterey, California. As luck would have it, his orders were changed, and he wound up being stuck at Fort Ord for a few extra months. Without a place to put him, the Army sent him to the Mechanics School on the base.

While he had often demonstrated a knack for mechanics, it was his ability to make money that came naturally to the young Mihaylo. At Fort Ord, he started tailoring uniforms and soon found he was making an extra $1,000 a month.

> *"I noticed everyone had all these baggy clothes, and they always wanted to get them tailored. This was while I was still in basic training. I went to a pawnshop and bought a sewing machine for $15 or $20. I experimented on my own clothes and got to where I was fairly good at tailoring, and I was making about $1,000 a month tailoring recruits' clothes for them in basic training."*[24]

The order mix-up at Fort Ord also bought Steve enough time to think about his future, and he volunteered for the 101st Airborne at Fort Campbell, Kentucky. While stationed at Fort Campbell, Steve found himself amid the escalating racial tensions in the South. In 1962, his division was sent to ensure that James Meredith, the first black man enrolled in the University of Mississippi, was permitted to attend his classes. "When we drove into town, we got a taste of what it was going to be like because they were throwing all sorts of things at us," Mihaylo said. "They were throwing bottles and rocks, tomatoes and fruit and things like that. It was scary."[25]

Shortly after that, his unit went on alert during the Berlin Wall crisis. It was months before the tension subsided.

Despite the excitement, Mihaylo was still looking forward to his discharge from the service. About a year before his run of duty was up, he saw an announcement on the bulletin board in company headquarters for an opening at the Army radio and radar technicians school. He later said that the appeal in transferring to the Southeast Signal School in Fort Gordon, Georgia, was to get out of the woods and off the muddy and cold ground on which he was forced to sleep.

> *"When you're part of an infantry division, even though we were the mechanics, you had to go out with these guys, and we were always on maneuvers, sleeping in tents in the middle of the forest somewhere out there in Kentucky or Tennessee. … The appeal of going to radio school was to get out of going on bivouac."[26]*

The Southeast Signal School provided Steve with a solid year of classroom instruction eight hours a day, five days a week, and in one year he earned the equivalent of a two-year engineering degree. In his three-year hitch in the Army, he spent most of his time in a classroom. Six months after graduating from the Southeast Signal School, he was released from the Army. With little direction, Steve set his sights on Phoenix, Arizona, or Houston, Texas, two growing cities with a lot of opportunity. "I decided I was going to go to either Houston or Phoenix and literally just flipped a coin, and Phoenix won," he said.[27]

Phoenix

In an old, white post office truck that he had painted himself and with a red trailer in tow, Steve moved from Kentucky into a trailer park across the street from Arizona State University in Tempe, Arizona. In need of a job, he headed for the employment office and was hired by Western Electric, the manufacturing arm of AT&T.

During the Cold War, Western Electric was contracted by the government to maintain its hardened-L communications system — an underground communications system that was designed to withstand the direct hit of a nuclear bomb. With his military and communications background, Steve was sent to work on the hardened-L carrier sites throughout the West.

While working in the field, Steve earned a reputation as a problem-solver and was promoted to field service engineer. He found scant fulfillment and little challenge in his new position, however, and after two years of moving throughout the Southwest for Western Electric, he grew restless. He recalled, "I felt like I could do just about anything, but Western Electric was like the military. You had to spend time in grade before they'd move you to the next level."[28]

Steve's mother's influence was strong. Anne Mihaylo believed in education. She was a voracious reader and adult student who urged her sons into school. Steve decided he wanted to get his college degree. Steve called his brother, Chuck, to ask for some advice. "I said, 'Steve, we're all going to be businessmen someday,'" Chuck remembered. "'The best thing we can do is to understand financial statements. So go ahead and major in accounting and finance.' Which Steve did."[29]

Eager to finish his degree, Steve enrolled in college carrying 22 to 24 credits per semester. After his stint with Western Electric, he had moved to California, so he attended both Orange Coast College and California State University, Fullerton, completing the four-year degree in two-and-a-half years. He majored in accounting, and he gained an understanding of how balance sheets work and how the flow of inventory and receivables affects the health of a business.

The hectic school schedule was compounded by a full-time job. During his first year of college, he worked the graveyard shift at Douglas Aircraft in Long Beach as a tube bender and welder. He recalled, "I'm lucky I didn't lose a finger or something in one of those machines, because if you'd fallen asleep at the machine, your clothing could have gotten into it."[30]

During his second year of college, Steve answered a small classified ad for an intercom installer and repairman at Panoramic Audio. The company's owner, Conway Chester, was impressed with the hardworking Mihaylo and agreed to let him work between classes and at odd hours. Chester recalled, "He was a great technician and did a great job. The kind of equipment we were using was a little bit unfamiliar to him, and he grasped it right away, very quick."[31]

In January 1969, Steve graduated from California State University, Fullerton, and was offered a job as an accountant with Arthur Young. "I was all set to become a green eye-shade accountant," he later recalled.[32] Steve accepted the job as accountant but decided to wait until the end of the summer before he started. In the meantime, Conway Chester gave Steve the opportunity to try his hand at selling intercom systems. Because he had no real sales experience, Conway sent him to a sales training class. In a hotel room in downtown Los Angeles, Steve took his first formalized sales training from a then-unknown Larry Wilson. Wilson would later publish five sales books and found the Pecos River Learning Centers.

Chester also introduced Steve to Craig Dorsey, who owned a large intercom distribution company in northern California. Dorsey's company was California's largest distributor of Ericsson Centrum intercom systems and represented several other equipment manufacturers. Hoping to grow his business, Chester traveled to San Francisco, where Dorsey tutored him in a five-step sales process. Dorsey remembered the method:

> *"It was very, very aggressive selling. We would get on the telephone and make appointments; then we would get a prospective customer to allow us to come in and do a telephone survey. We'd look at the telephone bills. We'd count the number of flashing lights. In those days, you paid for each flashing light. You paid for the hold button and all that, and we would do a complete telephone analysis to determine if we could come up with a better system at a lower cost."[33]*

Since value wasn't a priority with AT&T, it usually wasn't difficult to locate potential savings. The clients, however, didn't like to pay for intangibles, meaning they were usually unwilling to split their savings with Dorsey and his company. To make money, Dorsey would enter into a consulting agreement with the client and recommend intercom hardware that included such features as call distribution, personnel location and internal communications. If the customer was interested, Dorsey leased the equipment to him or her, installed it and waived the consulting fee.

This is the same sales method Chester taught to Mihaylo. Almost overnight, it seemed, Mihaylo had taken to sales like a fish to water. It was a natural progression for the young man, who as a boy had broken the *Los Angeles Herald Examiner* subscription record. He would never wear the green eye-shade awaiting him at Arthur Young. As his brother Matthew remembered, "The CPA job was going to start in September, but he had already made in the winter and spring more money than he would have made his first year at the CPA firm. So he decided that maybe selling was better."[34]

Inter-Tel's first phone system, the Key-Lux, launched the young business into the telecommunications industry.

CHAPTER FIVE

THE FIRST YEARS

"For the first four or five years, I would get up every morning and I didn't know if we'd be in business the next day or not. I just had to push through my fear. I couldn't give up; I pushed through my fears."

— Steve Mihaylo[1]

SELLING INTERCOM SYSTEMS THAT WINTER AND summer changed Steve Mihaylo's life. The 25-year-old proved himself to be a salesman par excellence. Furthermore, he had discovered that he had no great love for accounting. He had realized that advancement up the corporate ladder at Arthur Young, as in the U.S. Army and at Western Electric, would have been plodding and methodical, a concept that no longer appealed to him.

At Conway Chester's small intercom company, however, Mihaylo was operating in a fast-moving business where opportunities were limitless. Later in his career, his colleagues would credit Mihaylo with a tremendous sense of vision, but his decision to remain in telecommunications — one of the most important he would ever make — was more a matter of timing and luck.

"When I started Inter-Tel, it was difficult to envision the future," he remarked more than 20 years later. "The convergence of voice transmission and data transmission was not evident. Pursuing business was much more conscious than understanding the dynamics that were going on at the time I started Inter-Tel. It just happened that I had to make up my mind to go into accounting or do something else, and Conway Chester offered me a job selling. It was as much a case of circumstances as just being in the right place at the right time."[2]

Mihaylo didn't have to wait long. He approached one of Panoramic Audio's suppliers, Erik Daumstedder, and arranged to become a distributor of the Stentafone, a Norwegian-made intercom. At the first meeting, which took place in a swanky Los Angeles hotel, Mihaylo was impressed by the opulence of his surroundings, and his mind was made up. He wanted to work for himself.

When it came to choosing a location for his business, however, Mihaylo was unwilling to go into direct competition with his former boss. It would be unethical and run against his personal belief in loyalty. After all, Chester had helped him get started and therefore Mihaylo owed him a debt of gratitude. Since Mihaylo had lived in Phoenix, he reasoned it would be a good city for his new business and prepared to move.

Before he left, Chester convinced him he would need financial support to make his business viable. With this piece of advice, Mihaylo relocated to Phoenix and registered a new entity called Inter-Tel, a division of Panoramic Audio, on July 15, 1969. Five days later Apollo 11 landed on the moon, and Neil Armstrong made history's most famous footprint. In the new business, the Chesters — Conway and his wife Nancy — were registered as 50 percent partners with Steve Mihaylo.

When Mihaylo arrived back in Phoenix, the city's transformation from a dusty cowtown to a thriving metropolis was in full swing. From 1950 to 1969, Phoenix's population surged from 106,818 to 546,000,[3] making it one of the fastest growing cities in the booming Sun Belt. Hopeful job seekers looking to escape the difficult economic conditions in declining snowbelt cities flocked to Phoenix in droves.[4]

Industry flocked to the desert city as well. Drawn by the cheap labor, low cost of living and hospitable tax structure, companies such as Digital, Litton, ITT, General Semiconductors, Honeywell, Intel and GTE joined established Phoenix companies like Motorola, Sperry-Phoenix, General Electric and AiResearch. By 1969, manufacturing surpassed agriculture as the city's leading source of income.[5]

Along with opportunity, the swelling population brought its share of problems. In 1967, Phoenix possessed just 22 freeway miles for 500,000 people. Comparable cities such as Sacramento had 34 freeway miles for 300,000 people and San Diego, with 600,000 people, had 74 miles.[6]

As industrial expansion and economic growth claimed the cotton fields, cattle ranches and citrus orchards, Phoenix's political and business climate also changed. Once a town where "half a dozen men could sit down for lunch at the Arizona Club's round table and make decisions on new city projects,"[7] Phoenix struggled to form a central business establishment.[8] The distribution of power shifted away from the old guard to a new generation of leaders composed mostly of transplanted branch office managers and a handful of Big Board companies.

As the city shed the ways of old Phoenix, a doorway of opportunity opened for young companies and entrepreneurs looking to make a start. As Arizona Governor Bruce Babbitt put it, "If you've got a burning ambition to do something, in Phoenix there's absolutely no limits."[9]

This volatile mix of opportunity and risk was the right fit for Mihaylo, who was on uncertain financial ground and survived by wits and credit cards. He rented a room from an elderly woman in central Phoenix and a small office north of Indian School Road on 27th Avenue. For a desk, he found an old door in the alley and nailed it to the wall with two-by-fours. "Except for the fact that pencils and things would roll through the hole where the doorknob had been, it worked fairly well," he recalled.[10]

Thus set up, Mihaylo threw himself headlong into his new company. On his first day of cold calling, he hit upon an enormous opportunity. Canyon Ford, a car dealership on the corner of Thomas Road and Grand Avenue, was in need of a more efficient intercom system. As one of the state's largest dealerships, Canyon Ford represented 120 intercom units, a sale larger than Mihaylo had ever handled. If he could close the deal, not only would he have made his largest sale, but he would break Panoramic Audio's previous sales records.

But the owner of Canyon Ford, Perry Logan, and his general manager, Bent Pedersen, were a little hesitant to buy such an important and expensive system from someone with few credentials and no apparent service organization. Mihaylo spent more than a month convincing Logan and Pedersen that he could fulfill their internal communications system needs. He even flew them out to California to look at Panoramic Audio's systems and to prove he was legitimate. In the end, Mihaylo secured the deal and Inter-Tel made its first sale to Canyon Ford in the amount of $40,000.

With revenue coming in, Mihaylo could afford to replace the door nailed to the wall with a desk bought at auction.

"It was an old railroad desk where two people used to sit facing each other. There were drawers on

both sides of it. I bought it for about $20. It was a big oak desk. The thing was heavy. I took a Skil saw and I cut it in half and nailed two-by-fours to the back for legs. Then I had two desks."[11]

The sale also introduced Mihaylo to a lifelong friend, Perry Logan. Within a few months of closing their first deal, Logan, a private pilot, took Steve Mihaylo flying. Shortly after, Mihaylo began taking flying lessons. Over the years, Logan would continue buying phone systems from Inter-Tel, acting as a kind of beta tester for the latest phone systems.

Mihaylo's second sale was to KOY Radio at 840 North Central Ave. Bill Bosse, KOY's general manager, recalled how Mihaylo approached him: "Maybe six months after I was made general manager of the station, Steve walked in and said, 'Could you let me see your last year's telephone bills? I'll show you how you can have a better internal communication system than you now have and save some money.' So I said 'What the heck? What have I got to lose?'"[12]

Like many managers of small-sized to mid-sized companies, Bosse was dissatisfied with AT&T's Private Branch Exchange (PBX). In the late 1960s and early 1970s, AT&T's PBXs were notoriously sluggish and clunky systems unsuited for central dictation systems, closed-circuit televisions or loudspeaker paging devices.[13]

"I was never a big fan of those PBXs because they didn't offer a lot of flexibility," Bosse recalled. "I remember the first time we got one, we went from the six-button keysets to the PBX sets, and all of a sudden, you couldn't just pick up a phone anywhere and answer the phone after hours. I said something at the time like, 'This is progress?'"[14]

Using the consulting sales technique he and Chester had learned from Craig Dorsey, Mihaylo took the stack of bills into an office and analyzed them. He came back to Bosse's office with good news. By switching to the Norwegian-manufactured intercom system that Mihaylo was selling, Bosse would certainly realize savings. Bosse was interested.

"He did the analysis and he came in and said, 'Now I have this thing called a Stentafone. It's a touch-dial intercom system.' It was a nice looking gray and black unit with the louvered grill that just sat on the side of your desk. He said, 'We'll get rid of that big PBX out there and we'll put keysets all over.' Everything he said made a lot of sense to me because I liked the keysets in the first place. So I asked him who was going to install this, and he answered, 'I will.' I don't recall exactly what evening, but he came and installed it one night. He did all the work himself. I kind of liked him and got to know him. The system worked like a charm. In fact, it was still working when I left there three years later."[15]

That Mihaylo ran a one-man business didn't bother Bosse because "his word was good. Ultimately, that's the only thing that matters anyway." The two also became friends, and occasionally Mihaylo would have dinner at Bosse's house. Later, Bosse would stand as best man in Steve Mihaylo's wedding.

Within a matter of months after that second sale, Mihaylo was ready to move Inter-Tel out of the office on 27th Avenue. He approached Bosse for space. The KOY building happened to have open office space. Inter-Tel moved into a first-floor office with a private entrance and frontage on Central Avenue.

Now with a new office and two satisfied customers, Inter-Tel was becoming established in Phoenix. The timing was perfect. It was 1970 and the Carterfone decision issued by the FCC suddenly opened a door into the telephone interconnect equipment business. Soon, Mihaylo sold his first pure phone system to Frank Lewis, a Phoenix attorney.

He followed that by returning to his first two customers, Bosse and Logan, and sold phone systems to both of them. His business was booming in an industry that was doing the same.

Competing in the Market

Despite AT&T's best efforts to quash its tiny competitors, the interconnect industry boomed. From July 15, 1969, to November 30, 1969, Mihaylo did $90,000 in intercom sales — just enough to break even. With some money coming in, Mihaylo next turned his attention to buying Conway Chester's stake in Inter-Tel. At the time, Chester's stake in Inter-Tel was worth $25,000 — money that Mihaylo didn't have. He approached a friend, Dave Caldwell, who ran a division of Eaton Industries called Equilease. "Dave said, 'Is there anything you can come up with that's an asset to borrow against?' I said, 'No, we haven't been in business that long, and whatever there is, a finance company owns!'"[16]

What Mihaylo did have, however, was a five-year lease signed by one of his customers. Using that lease as collateral, Caldwell was able to work out an arrangement to loan Mihaylo the money, which Mihaylo used to buy out the Chesters.

Although it took some cajoling for Chester to release his profitable hold over Inter-Tel, the split was generally amicable. By this time, Mihaylo had begun to realize he could turn Inter-Tel into a multimillion-dollar business but needed the freedom of self-ownership to do it. Also, according to Chester, the two men had a difference in philosophy. Like many small business owners, the Chesters were happy to run a private business and live very comfortable lives. Mihaylo, on the other hand, had a much more ambitious business plan, remembered Chester.

> *"Steve's outlook after he had graduated from college with his accounting background was one in which he had interest in going public. I would travel to Arizona one week out of the month and dedicate my time there to training sales personnel and working with Steve. But over a period of a couple of years, my values were such that I preferred to stay in Southern California where I lived as opposed to traveling all over the country. Steve has a chemistry that is more friendly to that lifestyle, and he also has an education that allowed him to comprehend and understand the way in which to work with a public business structure. So the decision was made to go our separate ways, and he was 100 percent on his own."[17]*

As he took over Inter-Tel, Mihaylo continued to grow his company. He had hired his first employee, secretary Karen Johnson, in the first month of doing business. Ray Underell, his first salesman, joined a couple months later. "[Ray] actually came in to sell me a copy machine," Mihaylo said. "It was the first copier we bought, or one of the first ones we bought, and I was so impressed with him that I hired him."[18] Underell sold Inter-Tel products for several years before moving out of the state.

With his first employees coming on board, Mihaylo began to confront issues that every employer faces: how to keep the workforce motivated and satisfied, how to keep people focused and excited about their work. Already known for working long hours, Mihaylo knew he wanted to run a disciplined company — but not an intimidating one. He wanted the work to be fun and mutually rewarding, with Inter-Tel returning to its employees the loyalty and dedication they showed the company.

The resulting organization was set up as a surrogate family, and in later years, Inter-Tel would often be called Mihaylo's second family. Beginning its first year in business, Inter-Tel sponsored Christmas parties, company picnics and sent out Thanksgiving turkeys. When a baby was born, Inter-Tel sent a gift certificate to celebrate the occasion. Mihaylo also began a tradition that grew as the years went by — on every employee's birthday, he sent a personalized card with a handwritten message.

The reporting structure in the young company was deliberately relaxed. Everybody knew what needed to be done, and peer pressure was a tremendous motivator because, in a small organization, the whole company suffered if someone wasn't carrying his or her weight. Mihaylo himself preferred to manage by consensus rather than dictums handed down in memos.

A unified front was essential to survive in the rancorous business climate of the day, with hundreds of start-ups vying for position in the fledgling interconnect business. Since there were no domestic phone system manufacturers except AT&T, all the companies represented foreign equipment. In a 1972 *Electronic News* article, estimates were that the industry would reach $2.2 billion by 1980.[19] The article also cited a market research report by Frost & Sullivan claiming that "now is the most 'opportune time' for entering or expanding into the telephone equipment interconnect market."

By 1973, more than 250 interconnect companies were competing for customers, although fewer than a dozen controlled between 85 percent and 90 percent of the market. As an article in *Barron's* weekly newspaper noted, "Lucrative as the business may be for some, it is filled with pitfalls for others. For one thing, it is highly fragmented, with more than

250 competitors, most of them small three- and four-man shops. Price-cutting is rampant and has been responsible for more than a few firms filing for Chapter XI."[20]

The article went on: "Within the next year or so, there will be an unbelievable shakeout. Only the companies that know the industry and have the capital will survive. But those that do survive will be stronger."[21]

Mihaylo was determined to emerge stronger. At times like this, Mihaylo was inspired by personal heroes. He read biographies compulsively and drew inspiration from his mother, John F. Kennedy and Winston Churchill. With Churchill's "fight in the streets" mentality, Mihaylo approached his business as a long-distance runner approaches the Olympics. He worked 12-hour days, seven days a week. Bosse remembered that "he was so focused on that business and so consumed by it that he really didn't have much time for anything else and didn't do much of anything else."[22]

He was driven as much by fear as by determination. "Those first years I would wake up every morning and I didn't know if we'd be in business the next day or not," Mihaylo remembered during a 1997 interview. "I had to push through my fear. I couldn't give up; I pushed through my fears. You have to keep pushing forward until you get through; it's no different today. I still have that same fear in the pit of my stomach."[23]

Success, however, wasn't guaranteed by long hours and hard work. What customers wanted were features. They wanted capabilities that previously had been unavailable to small businesses from the giant AT&T systems. To accommodate this need, Mihaylo approached manufacturers and asked them to design additional features into their telephone systems.

"I'd say, 'My customers want more features, and now that they can own their own telephone system, they want to buy something that's better than AT&T's. Could you add this? Could you add that?' They'd say, 'Look, we've been doing it this way for 50 years. We don't need some 26-year-old kid to tell us what to do. If you're so smart, why don't you do it yourself?' "[24]

Steve Goes to Japan

The challenge struck a chord. Perhaps, Mihaylo thought, Inter-Tel could do it alone. If his current manufacturers were unwilling to make adjustments to their products, he would find someone who was. With that aim in mind, he set out in search of new systems vendors.

During his phone installation at the law firm, Mihaylo had been impressed by Nippon Electric. The huge company had flown an engineer from Japan on short notice to help him install a single phone system. Based on that first experience, Mihaylo decided that Japan would be a good place to look for a manufacturing partner. He obtained a list of several hundred Japanese equipment manufacturers from Frank Woods at the Phoenix office of the U.S. Commerce Department, contacted each one on the list, singled out 20 based on their responses, and in September 1971 boarded a plane bound for Japan.

When he boarded the plane, the 28-year-old had never been out of the United States except to Mexico and a short trip to England. Nor did he have any knowledge of the Japanese language or the intricate web of custom that dictates Japanese business practices. "It was scary," he remembered. "Before boarding the flight to Japan, I bought a little book, Learn Japanese Quick or something like that. I memorized all the phrases like 'thank you' and 'good morning' and 'good afternoon' and how to count. It was the early seventies, just when commerce was really getting started between the United States and Japan."[25]

Fortunately, Mihaylo quickly developed contacts who could help. On one of his many subsequent trips to Asia, he met and befriended a Japanese-American named Sen Nishiyama. As a Japanese-American who had lived in both countries, Nishiyama was a valuable source of information. Although he had grown up in Ogden, Utah, after the death of his father, he attended college in Japan. In many ways, his college experience taught him more than he could have ever expected. While he was a student, World War II broke out, and Nishiyama was drafted into the Japanese army. Although he was an American citizen, he was bilingual and became a Japanese citizen. After the war, he soon found himself in the position of main liaison between General MacArthur and the Japanese government during the postwar occupation. More than 20 years later, he left the government and landed a job setting up international operations for Sony Corporation.

Mihaylo would often rely on Nishiyama as Asia became more important to Inter-Tel in the years that followed. Whenever he ran into a problem with a Japanese supplier, he turned to Nishiyama for advice. "He was a great guy to learn about the culture and understand the people because he was totally bicultural and bilingual," remarked Mihaylo.[26]

Once in Japan, Mihaylo began searching for a telephone system manufacturer that would work with him. He finally settled on Taiko Electric Works. At Taiko, he found a system he thought could run circles around his American competitors. Furthermore, Taiko agreed to give Mihaylo control over the manufacture and design of his products. It was the start of a long and prosperous relationship.

"Taiko had what I thought was a gorgeous phone at the time. It had a lot of great features. We started importing it. I went out and sold or pledged everything

I had and borrowed as much as possible and bought a warehouse full of this equipment.

"At just about the same time, one of my competitors by the name of TIE [Telephone Interconnect Equipment] was importing equipment from Japan too, from another company by the name of Nitsuko. They were pretty big by then. They had grown in just a few short years from zero to probably $50 million or $100 million in sales. Nitsuko had this ugly looking phone, and the one from Taiko was beautiful, and I thought, 'I'm going to just do miracles. I'm going to knock the daylights out of them.'"[27]

When he returned to the U.S., Mihaylo hired Craig Dorsey and his associate, Bob Knudsen, to sell the new Key-Lux telephone, as Mihaylo called it. Dorsey, who had once mentored Chester and Mihaylo, now owned a company called American International Telephone in San Francisco. "Craig Dorsey looked at this phone and said, 'This is great. We can sell this to dealers,'" Mihaylo remembered.[28]

Their enthusiasm, however, was short-lived. Features and style sold systems, and the new Key-Lux soon lacked style and a critical new feature that the competition had just introduced. A month after the Key-Lux telephone hit the market, TIE introduced a newly redesigned and stylish telephone with hands-free answer-back — a feature similar to a speaker phone that allowed the user to speak into the intercom system without picking up the handset.

In an industry driven by demand for practical features, Mihaylo found himself with a warehouse full of telephones and systems that wouldn't sell because they didn't offer the latest advance and, to top it off, were ugly compared to TIE's sleek new system. The Key-Lux had become outdated by one quick jump of the competition. As 1973 approached, Mihaylo found himself saddled with a warehouse full of inventory and dangerously close to failure.

The Key-Lux phone boasted a smaller cable than its competitors, which allowed customers to reduce desk clutter. Nevertheless, it was an uphill battle to establish a phone that was quickly leap-frogged by the competition.

CHAPTER SIX

STRAW INTO GOLD

"When I showed the ugly telephone to prospective dealers, I'd say, 'This is our European designer model.' And I'd show people how durable it was. I'd throw it on the floor as hard as I could and the telephone would take it."

— Steve Mihaylo[1]

ITH $2.5 MILLION TIED UP IN AN INVENTORY of telephones that would not sell, Inter-Tel teetered dangerously close to bankruptcy. Because the company relied on the Key-Lux, Mihaylo had little choice but to push for sales even though Inter-Tel competed against a better looking TIE telephone with better features. "The TIE phone had become the stylish one and ours was now the dog," Mihaylo remembered.[2]

To make matters worse, Craig Dorsey and Bob Knudsen decided to leave after only a couple of months. "They came to me and said, 'This telephone is the ugliest looking thing around. We can't sell this.' I was left with a warehouse full of inventory. I thought, 'Oh God, what am I going to do now?'"[3]

Dorsey, who characterized the split as a "friendly divorce," was a successful businessman and a good salesman but remembers that he couldn't sell Mihaylo's phone. "It was a good system," Dorsey said. "But it was probably the ugliest telephone system that was ever built."

"People would just gasp when you'd take it out of your little bag. I thought I was a pretty good salesman, but I was not successful selling that. ... I was out of the intercom era. I had sold a lot of intercoms with hands-free-answer-back. I was a believer in being on an outside call and being able to place an internal call without putting you on hold, and that was a real key part of our whole sales program."[4]

It was left to Mihaylo to sell the inventory himself, and selling the Key-Lux phone system would consume him for the next 18 months. Mihaylo pushed himself at a punishing pace to sell off the telephones.

"On Sunday night, I'd fly into a city like Cincinnati. I'd get there at about 1 a.m. Then I'd drive to Lexington, Kentucky, for a 6 a.m. breakfast with a prospective dealer, then I'd drive to Louisville, Kentucky, to have an 8 or 8:30 a.m. breakfast with another prospective dealer. Then I'd drive all the way to Cleveland and have lunch there. Then I'd start my trek back south again through Dayton and Columbus and wind up in Cincinnati for dinner. Then I'd fly to the next city, maybe New York, and I'd drive up to Albany, do three or four stops there, and then I'd drive over to Boston, drive down to Baltimore and Washington and Virginia and wind up back in New York that night. These were all 24-hour trips. That would be Tuesday. Then Wednesday, I'd do the same thing down in Georgia or some place or in the Carolinas, and then on

Thursday, I'd do it down in Texas, and I'd be back in Phoenix on Thursday night after seeing 30 or 40 dealers in a four-day period. When I'd turn the car back in, there'd be 1,000 or 1,200 miles on it in each 24-hour period. Sometimes the car rental agent would check the odometer three or four times in disbelief. On Friday, I'd sell in Phoenix to end users and then over the weekend, I'd install the sales myself on Saturday and Sunday before I left again to hit the dealer trail. I did that for 18 months."[5]

At the same time, he knew the Key-Lux would have to be upgraded. In 1974, however, the industry wasn't waiting for Inter-Tel to work out its problems. Other companies were quickly adding features to their systems, and Inter-Tel's Key-Lux risked becoming obsolete. Both the Key-Lux and Inter-Tel's other product, a PBX called the Centurion, lacked Touch-Tone dials, which allowed the use of Touch-Tone phones, a novelty introduced by AT&T in 1963 that was on its way to becoming the standard.

While it was possible to modify the phones, Mihaylo didn't have the necessary equipment. Already on uncertain ground, there was no way Inter-Tel could afford to buy Touch-Tone dials at $15 apiece. Then he met with an unexpected piece of good luck. Litton Industries, a massive conglomerate based in California, was shutting down its phone manufacturing company and wanted to sell off its inventory. This included about 15,000 Touch-Tone dials that Litton was willing to unload for $1 each. Mihaylo jumped at the opportunity.

"They had a warehouse in the Bay area, so I went there to look at them," he remembered. "Nobody wanted these dials, but it was just the ticket for me. I spent just about all the spare cash I had, but then I didn't have any way to get them back to Phoenix because I didn't have any money left to have them shipped."[6]

Necessity being the mother of invention, he packed the dials into hundreds of boxes and began checking them through San Francisco's airport to Phoenix as luggage. It took him three days, two boxes at a time, to check all the dials through. He arrived in Phoenix shortly after his coveted dials and then repeated the entire procedure to get them to Japan, where Taiko was waiting to modify the old hardware with Touch-Tone equipment.

"It was a little trickier to get them to Japan, and it took me a week to send them over," Mihaylo said. "When I got there, they were waiting for me. Every single one of them made it, and the Japanese were amazed because they just couldn't believe I sent all that stuff ahead."[7]

In the short run, this saved a couple thousand dollars that Inter-Tel didn't have and demonstrated the kind of tenacity that kept the business afloat. In the long run, however, Inter-Tel needed a more permanent fix to engineering problems. Mihaylo's search for a solution led him away from Arizona, which wasn't yet a technology center, to the East Coast, where an answer presented itself in the form of an engineer named Gerhardt Klaiber, who had done work for TIE. Klaiber introduced him to another engineer named Tom Peiffer.

Mihaylo approached Peiffer at an opportune moment. Peiffer had experience designing Touch-Tone receivers, which allowed a telephone system to receive the signals that the Touch-Tone dials generate, and he was looking for a job. Peiffer was a design engineer for Klaiber's company in New Jersey. The company was in financial trouble and had "laid off just about the entire work force in one day."[8] According to Peiffer, Klaiber "felt guilty" about laying everybody off and put him in touch with Mihaylo.

For his initial interview, Mihaylo flew Peiffer out to Phoenix and hosted the engineer and his wife at his house rather than springing for a hotel room. Fortunately, the unorthodox practice didn't unsettle Peiffer.

"It was a very small company, and Steve had us stay at his house. He didn't want to put us up in a hotel. So we just stayed in one of his bedrooms, and the next day we went over to the office, which was downtown in a radio station building. You'd come in from the back parking lot, and Inter-Tel had a little

Shown in 1977, Tom Peiffer joined Inter-Tel in 1974. He spent his first three years at the company redesigning the Key-Lux.

PHOTO COURTESY OF N. THOMAS PEIFFER.

parking area reserved, and then you'd walk in this
back door and go down a couple steps and you're in
the lower level, where he had a sales office set up and
one technician who was working on phone systems. It
was like walking into a small car dealer."[9]

There were no other engineers. There was no lab. In
fact, there were almost no facilities at all and a gigantic
challenge waiting for any incoming talent. Yet Peiffer decided to accept the position. Not only was he ready to move
out of New Jersey, but Mihaylo offered Peiffer a salary that
beat the three or four others he had previously received
and the chance for the engineer to break new ground.
Inter-Tel's first engineer moved from New Jersey to Arizona
in late April and reported for work on May 6, 1974.

"I hired Tom and I said, 'Tom, we've got to add some
features,'" Mihaylo remembered. "'Our systems need
Touch-Tone dialing.'"[10]

Peiffer spent his first months designing Touch-Tone
receivers for the system. Throughout the redesign, Inter-
Tel worked closely with Taiko, sending the Japanese
company crude drawings that Taiko mechanical engineers turned into working products.

Even before the Centurion receiver project was completed, Peiffer turned his attention to the rather unique
demands of the Key-Lux, which lacked the popular
hands-free answer-back. To remedy that, he installed a
voice-activated circuit connected to a speaker.

"Steve had bought an awful lot of inventory, and
he thought we would be able to go out without hands-
free answer-back. It turned out we couldn't. The mar-
ket would not buy the phones without that feature. So
technicians spent quite a few months working through
that inventory pulling the phones apart and putting a

conversion in them to make them hands-free answer-back, putting them back in the boxes and putting them in inventory."[11]

The next modification to the Key-Lux was designed to make it easier to customize to individual customer wants. To add phones or lines in the Key-Lux system meant tediously unwrapping and rewrapping wire, meaning it wasn't easily altered. Many of Inter-Tel's competitors, however, offered phone systems that were modular and had plug-in cards, similar to modern PCs. Peiffer corrected this by "taking a cookie-cutter approach and drawing dotted lines on all the circuits that were connected into the base unit, adding several new features and making S.S.I. logic-based printed circuit cards so they would just plug in."[12] This improvement doubled the capacity of the system from 30 to 60 phones and was introduced as the next-generation Key-Lux II.

"We originally purchased the Key-Lux telephone system from Taiko Electric Works, and the control box that ran the system was a 1960s design where you slid the front panel off and everything was on a hinge and folded out. If you wanted to replace something in the system, you had to unwire all the connectors on it with a little wiring tool. Then you had to delicately pull the part out and replace it."[13]

These upgrades made Mihaylo happy because his phone's cable was half as large as the Bell system's cable, so he could boast that his system offered all the advantages of the Bell system, without the big cable. Ray McCloud began installing Key-Lux II telephones for Inter-Tel in 1976. "The Key-Lux II was pretty revolutionary for the industry back then," McCloud said. "It gave the customer the option of using several more lines on his telephone with only a 25-pair cable. Most other similar types of phones used a 50-pair cable."[14]

National Distribution

The resulting phone was narrow with rounded corners and looked vaguely European in its design. "Even though it was ugly, we had a set of features that nobody else had," Mihaylo remembered. "I used to take that ugly phone and I'd say, 'This is our European designer model.'"

"I would show people how durable it was. I'd throw it on the floor as hard as I could, and the phone would take it. The people I was selling to would say, 'Let me try that.' Then they'd smash the thing on the floor. Usually when I was traveling, I went through four or five phones like that because after about the eighth or ninth time, it would finally start to break, and inside it would start crumbling."[15]

Throughout the time that Peiffer upgraded, Mihaylo was constantly traveling and selling. "He was always playing the shell game," Peiffer remembered, "moving himself around."[16] Although he preferred direct sales offices, Mihaylo reasoned that authorized dealers were a good way to give Inter-Tel a quick boost. Ultimately a mix of dealers and direct sales offices would give Inter-Tel more control over its own destiny.

By 1974, Inter-Tel had 40 employees and had outgrown the old radio station. The company had installers, a sales force, secretaries and technicians, and it moved into a newly constructed, 10,000-square-foot building at 1420 N. 27th Avenue. Around this time, Inter-Tel set up a retirement plan for its employees. This was long before the 401K existed, and the only U.S. workers who had solid retirement plans were employees of large corporations or the government.

Mihaylo also set up a loose group of advisers that formed the company's first board of directors. Bill Oliver, an executive officer for a customer from Mihaylo's days in Southern California, was invited to be one of the first board members. "He wanted to put together a group of advisers that could assist him in business plans and growth," Oliver said. "He found people that he felt could make a contribution in various ways. Each of us that came into the board had a different background and was able to bring a nice mixture of background and experience."[17] Mihaylo believed that a board of outside directors could bring great benefit to his company and installed only himself and one other Inter-Tel insider on the panel.

Regardless of the company's momentum, Mihaylo's decision to set up direct sales offices was opposed by his management team and his new board of directors. Other start-up companies had tried national direct sales networks and failed. In an article for *Administrative Management*, one consultant wrote, "It's been proven beyond a reasonable doubt that companies relying on a nationwide direct sales network often don't make a go of it. Arcata, Litton, Rollins and United Business Communications are some of the companies who have taken this route and failed."[18]

Unlike Inter-Tel, however, these companies lacked tight financial controls, and Mihaylo was convinced that Inter-Tel's future depended on distribution at least as much as products. In 1975, as the inventory of Key-Lux telephones was finally emptying out, Mihaylo made an opportune connection at an industry trade show where he met a TIE salesman named Steve Sherman. Sherman remembers approaching the simple table where Mihaylo was standing in front of the Key-Lux. "He was a young man, still in his twenties, standing there with his phone that was so ugly," Sherman said. "But Steven thought it was beautiful, and that was all that really mattered."[19]

Sherman was one of TIE's first employees, and like Inter-Tel, TIE was one of the first companies to bring non-AT&T equipment to market. Based in New Jersey, Sherman had spent four years setting up a distribution network for the company. By the time he met Mihaylo he was director of sales at a company 25 times larger than Inter-Tel. Despite all that he had done at TIE, however, Sherman was not a shareholder and had no vested interest in the company. He was looking for a way to make even more money than a commissioned salesman, however successful, can make. In Mihaylo's business, he found the perfect opportunity.

Likewise, Mihaylo was happy to have Sherman's expertise, connections and energy. Since his first flying lessons, Mihaylo had become an aviation enthusiast and tirelessly criss-crossed the country in his single engine Cessna meeting with dealers and customers. In Sherman, he saw a way to go after TIE customers.

They "struck up a friendship," according to Sherman, and before long Mihaylo suggested they take a weekend trip to New Orleans with their wives to see if a business relationship would work.

The two men who were to become such close friends were very different. Mihaylo could never be described as "easygoing" while at work, but he was more reserved and quieter than the fast-talking, persuasive Sherman. During a crisis, Mihaylo's instinct was to calm down and focus relentlessly on his goal. Inter-Tel, he remarked, was the kind of company that "has the spirit to keep ramming against a wall until it collapses, for a 100 years if it's necessary."[20] An example of that tenacity was an informal weight loss competition at Inter-Tel in the 1970s. A couple of Inter-Tel employees put $20 in a pool to see who could lose the most weight. Mihaylo threw himself into the bet, taking it to the same extremes he used to sell phones. He went on a strict diet and began running. Before long, he had dropped from 174 pounds to 148 — significantly underweight.

Sherman, on the other hand, was more explosive and emotional. After Inter-Tel went public in 1981 and made them both rich men, Sherman celebrated by hanging his head out the window of a sports car going 70 mph and singing at the top of his lungs. Mihaylo invested in another business.

In 1976, Sherman signed on with Mihaylo at eight percent commission and began approaching his old TIE customers to switch them over to Inter-Tel products. Bill Nicewanger was one of the first dealers to make the switch. Nicewanger had founded an interconnect equipment distributor in Ohio in 1974 and signed on with Inter-Tel a couple years later. He was approached by Sherman, and he remembered his reasons for agreeing to take on the Inter-Tel product line.

"We had been selling TIE, and there were several different people selling TIE in the same marketplace. It seemed like the opportunity to distinguish ourselves with another product that at that instant may not have been much different from the TIE products because there was the hope that there would soon be another product that was different. Our decision to sell Inter-Tel also had something to do with the persuasiveness of the person calling on us."[21]

As the distribution network began to take shape, Sherman and Mihaylo spent more and more time together, working through problems as they came up. "We traveled all over the world together," Sherman remembered. During this marathon traveling, the two would often take a single hotel room to save money. Occasionally, one or the other would be forced to sleep on the floor. Soon, however, their efforts began to bear fruit as an Inter-Tel distribution network stretched across the nation. A major victory came in New Jersey, where Inter-Tel switched a TIE dealer named Barry Wichansky. Sherman recalled meeting Wichansky.

> "I remember the first time I took the Key-Lux out to Barry. He's in business with his brother and his father selling background music to businesses, and Barry also sold business phone systems. I took the phone out of the box to show it to them. Well, they didn't vomit, but his brother walked out of the room. I closed the box and Barry said, 'OK' and started giving me an order. I went home and told my wife what happened. I told her it was just awful. My wife says to me, 'So why do you show it to them?' From then on, I never took that phone out of the box. Ever."[22]

Wichansky agreed that he didn't sign with Inter-Tel because he was impressed with the Key-Lux systems. By the time Inter-Tel approached him, he was one of the largest TIE dealers in New Jersey and TIE was aggressive in its attempts to keep him, but Wichansky was impressed with the man behind Inter-Tel.

> "I really bought Steve Mihaylo, not even the product of Inter-Tel. He had a vision and had a real nice business plan even though TIE was so much larger at that time. TIE was very upset, and they wanted to know what they could do to get me back in the fold. They offered me all kinds of opportunities."[23]

Wichansky would not be swayed — he was already sold on Mihaylo's vision of the future of telephone equipment distribution. It was something that Mihaylo and Sherman disagreed on, but Sherman would later concede that Mihaylo was "probably right." Based on the successful TIE formula, Sherman believed that dealer/distributors were the best way to move product. Mihaylo, on the other hand, wanted to establish a balance of dealers and direct sales offices. At the time, most interconnect phone equipment was sold exclusively through small, independent dealer/distributors. Eventually, Mihaylo predicted, many of these dealerships would be replaced as their owners either closed their doors or sold their business to equipment suppliers like Inter-Tel. Wichansky, who followed this path when he sold his dealership to Inter-Tel years later, remembered Mihaylo's pitch.

"Steve had long-term vision. He realized to be successful in marketing private telephone systems, he would eventually have to control distribution. He recognized that before anybody else. The whole world thought he was wrong. If he kept just a dealer network, they were just a bunch of mom and pop operations. With mom and pop operations, they take everything out of their business and sooner or later, they end up getting in trouble. I saw that everything he said was right."[24]

The Problem with Direct Sales

Direct sales offices weren't without challenges, however. One of the major reasons so many companies opted exclusively for dealer networks is that they were a relatively easy way to quickly spread across the nation. In the "go-go" days of the industry, speed and market penetration were critical. A dealer simply had to like the product, place an order and take care of the rest. A direct sales office, on the other hand, required a major commitment from Inter-Tel. The company had to rent office space, staff it and deal with any personnel problems.

In Inter-Tel's first decade, Mihaylo established only three direct sales offices. The original Phoenix office was run by Jim Purdy. A smaller office in Tucson was run by Dan Smith. And, finally, there was an office in Denver that was so beset by problems it seemed the salesman was "selling $20 bills for $10."[25]

In late 1978, Mihaylo decided it was time to shake up the Denver office and, in January 1979, hired Craig Rauchle away from a local competitor called American Business Communications. As the director of sales and marketing for American Business Communications, Rauchle was used to selling against Inter-Tel and, at least in Denver, found it less than challenging.

"They had a crazy Dutch guy named Jeff Dyke, who was their only sales representative. He heavily discounted everything. Shotgun approach. No follow-up. No finesse. In competing against them, we would actually bring Inter-Tel into the deal. I was a Toshiba dealer at the time, and if the customer wanted to get three bids, my best-case scenario was to encourage the customer to get another bid from AT&T and if they wanted another interconnect, I would encourage them to call Inter-Tel. If they brought in Inter-Tel, I was confident I was going to close the deal because the salesperson was very predictable in what he would do and how he'd do it."[26]

Rauchle was hired to "put Inter-Tel on the map" in Denver. For his interview, he flew out to Mihaylo's house in Phoenix and saw the financials of Inter-Tel. "I was impressed with the company," he recalled. "Even though Inter-Tel was privately held and small, Steve ran it like a businessman, and that was in sync with what I was looking for at the time."[27]

When he came into the Denver office, there was only one salesman and a technical manager named Al Maynard. On slow afternoons, the employees gathered around a table in the back and actually played cards. That wouldn't last long. The employees got their warning that things were about to change when "Al went up to the technicians and said, 'Well, this new guy, I don't think he's going to like you playing cards in here anymore. He's kind of different.'"[28]

Part of the problem, Rauchle said, was that the Denver office viewed itself as a "step-child" in the Inter-Tel family. The office had no established goals, no drive and low expectations. Rauchle set himself to changing that perception.

"I had to create sales opportunities myself. Sell them. Come back, write orders at night, write the telco orders to get the telephone trunk lines switched. I'd sell it, close it, follow it up, order the equipment and coordinate everything. I was literally the chief cook and bottle washer."[29]

Recession and Recovery

During this critical period of Inter-Tel's development, the country plunged into a severe economic recession, putting serious financial strain on the company. As the gross national product dropped, inflation and unemployment rates soared. In 1975, *The New York Times* somberly reported, "It is by now practically certain that the current recession in the United States will be one of the longest since the 1930s. ... In some ways the recession is also proving to be one of history's deepest. Unemployment has well passed the 6 percent danger line. The list of industries in really depressed conditions is by no means confined to autos, appliances and housing but uncharacteristically includes even chemicals, which have long been considered recession-proof."[30]

The financial pressures became so stressful that Mihaylo briefly considered selling half of the company. His brother Andy recalled, "He was really hurting for some money. ... Steve said he would have sold half of Inter-Tel for $100,000."[31]

Fortunately for Inter-Tel, the situation wasn't permanent. The economy began to improve in the mid-1970s as Mihaylo steadily emptied the company's warehouse of Key-Lux telephone systems.

There were important lessons to be learned through this period of adversity. With his background in accounting, Mihaylo became a disciple of the balance sheet. Money that was tied up in inventory and receivables wasn't available for working capital. Furthermore, in the interconnect business, many of the mom and pop operations that sold Inter-Tel equipment used Inter-Tel as a bank. They bought equipment on open accounts and paid off Inter-Tel as they sold the phone systems. Mihaylo counteracted this by offering deep cash discounts. Still, the road to revenue wasn't always smooth.

"Most companies fail because they don't control their inventory and receivables," Mihaylo said.

"A lot of people think it's all profit and loss issues, but a lot of the profits and losses are generated on the balance sheet. Keep inventory as low as possible so you can't lose money on your inventory. With receivables, if your customers don't pay you, you wind up with bad

*debt and you go out of business. One of the problems
with setting up a distribution network is we found that
most of the dealers were all small businesses that were
undercapitalized. In some cases, we wound up with
dealers that couldn't pay, and I actually had to go out
and repossess inventory a few times. I would wait until
the owner went out to lunch, rent a van, then go in and
clean out his warehouse. I'd park the van maybe a mile
or two away, then go back, and I'd be sitting in the lobby
when the owner returned. If they came up with the
money, I brought back the inventory."[32]*

Back in Phoenix, flexibility was ingrained into the
company's engineering culture. Design innovations to
the Key-Lux systems didn't have to pass through layers
of management or committees; ideas flowed straight
from Peiffer to Mihaylo, and vice versa. Any weakness in
the distribution was spotted immediately and fixed. As
one industry observer noted, "Design innovations and
equipment modifications can be in the field three
weeks after inception by Inter-Tel while sometimes
Bell, because of size and regulatory complications, takes
three or four years."[33]

Inter-Tel also discovered its market niche. While the
majority of telephone equipment suppliers battled over
the larger business customers, Mihaylo focused on businesses with needs of less than 100 telephones. The Key-
Lux II was consciously designed to offer small to medium businesses access to "big system" features.

A reporter for *Today's Business* heralded the revamped
Key-Lux II as a system that "utilizes technology that bet-
ter-heeled competitors had been using for years in large
100 and 100-plus phone systems. Inter-Tel refined the
technology to fit small businesses who only need from four
to 20 telephones, offering greater reliability, longevity and

more call features than even the giant Bell system. All that for about the same monthly costs of renting from Bell — and you owned it after a few years to boot."[34]

The new and improved Key-Lux II was far from the poor stepchild it once had been. In 1975, Key-Lux II revenues pushed Inter-Tel past the $1 million highwater mark. By 1979, sales would reach $7.8 million, and the company could comfortably celebrate surviving the Key-Lux. Steve Mihaylo himself had sold the majority of the Key-Lux phone systems. Inter-Tel had also championed a unique position among its competitors. It was neither a manufacturer nor a distributor but a hybrid of both. While most interconnect companies scrambled to represent as many products as they could, Mihaylo had laid the groundwork for Inter-Tel to pioneer an innovative product line of its own.[35]

AT&T: Back in Court

Inter-Tel was able to compete in the interconnect industry through a combination of perseverance and good timing. The Carterfone decision had allowed the tiny company access to a huge market. In general, however, the telecommunications industry was unique among American industries in that it was almost totally controlled by a single company. Companies like Inter-Tel and TIE were simply nibbling away at AT&T's giant market share. But the rumbling that had begun with Carterfone was set to turn into an avalanche.

In 1974, the U.S. Department of Justice slapped AT&T with a second antitrust suit. Although it was yet another case in the seemingly endless litigation, this suit was particularly troubling for AT&T.

It was based on what the Department of Justice characterized as anti-competitive business practices. "The most specific of these charges," wrote author John Brooks in *Telephone: The First Hundred Years*, "concerned alleged attempts by AT&T to obstruct interconnection of competing terminal equipment and specialized-common-carrier equipment, all of which was technologically new since 1956."[36] AT&T was charged with monopolistic practices in the telephone equipment industry and with noncompliance with the Carterfone ruling.

The Department of Justice had an ambitious case. It wanted to increase competition by breaking Western Electric away from AT&T. In addition, the Justice Department called for the divestiture of some or all of the Bell operating companies. "In short, the Justice Department wanted AT&T to serve as nothing more than a long-distance company with some connection to Bell Labs," explained author Alan Stone in his book, *Wrong Number*.[37] If the government was successful, it would dismantle the nation's largest company.

For the next eight years, the telecommunications industry watched and waited as Ma Bell spent millions of dollars defending itself.[38]

The Key-Lux Key Service Unit. Inter-Tel's first software program using microprocessors designed a system to test the Key-Lux before it went out to customers.

CHAPTER SEVEN

THE MICROPROCESSOR

"Put as many of these features as you can inside our key telephone system and we'll sell them more competitively to small customers. We can make a fortune if the microprocessor is as powerful as we think it is."

— Steve Mihaylo's instructions to Tom Peiffer after showing the development team promotional material for large-scale PBX systems.[1]

T HE LATTER HALF OF THE 1970S WAS NOT A good time for AT&T. The company that had single-handedly driven communications technology for nearly a century was under intense pressure from the Justice Department, which was determined to break it up into smaller pieces. But it wouldn't be the Justice Department that toppled AT&T from its position atop pioneering communications technology. That distinction came from a wholly unexpected direction.

Prior to the mid-1970s, the technology emerging from what would become known as Silicon Valley had little impact on Inter-Tel. The last major advance in telephony infrastructure had been AT&T's introduction in 1965 of the No. 1 Electronic Switching System, which benefitted only large-scale systems. The No. 1 ESS replaced complicated electromechanical crossbar switching systems with an electronic version. It could serve as many as 65,000 two-way voice circuits and signaled the movement of telephony to solid-state components. Smaller customers, however, with internal phone and intercom systems had yet to benefit from digital technology.

By 1976, however, an innovation known as a microprocessor was making serious inroads into American industry. Introduced by Intel in 1971, microprocessors were tiny "smart" devices that used semiconductor technology to process information at blinding speed. The Intel 4004 was the first microprocessor introduced; it was followed quickly by the marginally improved 8008. These first chips were difficult to program and were nowhere near as powerful or as fast as the large mainframes of the day. Nevertheless, Intel co-founder Gordon Moore hailed the 4004 as "one of the most revolutionary products in the history of mankind."[2]

In 1974, Intel introduced the 8080 microprocessor, a manageable 8-bit chip priced between $5 and $50. Competition in the microprocessor industry was already fierce, with companies like Motorola, Texas Instruments and Zilog vying to beat Intel at its own game. The 8080 chip promised a revolution in both consumer goods and heavy industry. Gordon Moore's boast would be fulfilled over the ensuing decades, as microprocessors found their way into thousands of everyday products like calculators, desktop computers, industrial robots, the black boxes on airplanes, digital clocks, microwaves, cars and, most importantly for Inter-Tel, telephone systems.

Telephone systems, which were required to direct and control thousands of calls, were ripe for the microprocessor. Until the advent of the microprocessor, small companies like Inter-Tel had no control over their switching technology. They had to use electromechanical devices for their products or cede the business to AT&T. The microprocessor made it possible for Inter-Tel to envision an affordable telephone system that would offer small to medium businesses all the advantages of huge PBX systems.

Writing for *Telephony* magazine in 1976, Howard Bersted predicted, "In this centennial year you might reflect on the fact that more changes have occurred in our industry in the last eight years — starting with the Carterfone — than in the first 92 years of the industry's life. And, I'll wager, more significantly big changes in the telephone industry will happen in the next five years than in the previous 100."[3]

This statement proved absolutely correct.

"It was about 1977 that Tom Peiffer came to me and said, 'I think I can come up with a design to put microprocessors in the phone,'" Mihaylo said. "I answered, 'That sounds like a good idea. Let's see what you can do.'"[4]

Peiffer, as engineers are prone to do, felt anxious to see what the new device was capable of. But there was a problem: Peiffer had received his diploma in 1971, the year microprocessors were introduced. He had no experience with them.

"There was a lot of talk among my friends and in the newspapers. I started to catch word of this microprocessor industry, and everybody was saying that the microprocessor was going to replace wired logic and relays, the technology that we were using in the Key-Lux."[5]

To learn more about how microprocessors worked, Peiffer enrolled in microprocessor design classes at Arizona State University.[6]

"We started with the microprocessor to see if it could be of any use in our business. Some of our com-

petitors had already been talking about using these microcomputers in phone systems, saying they were going to replace the old computers that took up a whole room with just one circuit board. We were all excited about it."[7]

But the technology was still young and unproven, so Peiffer developed a program that eased Inter-Tel into the digital age. The first microprocessor project at Inter-Tel was "designed as a test machine running under stored program control to test existing Key-Lux production assemblies."[8]

At the time, Inter-Tel was still buying manufactured components from Taiko Electric Works in Japan. Microprocessors offered a natural opportunity to test both Inter-Tel products before shipment and the capabilities of the processor itself. Peiffer spent the summer of 1977 programming a Motorola 6801 chip to check the Key-Lux II for defects.

"We programmed a microprocessor to go out and probe the cards and ask if everything was working OK. After that was over, I said, 'This is really true because the microprocessors on this little card test this huge phone system. It's all compressed into a circuit card. And if I don't like the way it works, all I need to do is make a program change.' We instantly saw the power of being able to do that."[9]

Encouraged by its success, Inter-Tel committed more resources and time to microprocessor projects. In November 1977, a second engineer joined the company. Bill Ennist, an engineer with Goodyear Aerospace, responded to a small ad in the *Arizona Republic* for an engineer. For Ennist, the job meant a $6,000 pay cut, but he was looking to get out of the shaky defense industry.[10]

With a new round of layoffs every other year at Goodyear Aerospace, Ennist had little guarantee that his job would be around for long, and he was ready for a different environment. "At Inter-Tel, it looked like we could do a lot of good without having to go through all the red tape," Ennist said. "And we could focus on issues that we could really dedicate ourselves to."[11]

Although he was hired for the microprocessor program, his first project at Inter-Tel was to guarantee that the company's products met new FCC standards. One of these qualifications was that the equipment be able to withstand the surge created by a lightning strike. Since there were no standard test fixtures to simulate lightning strikes, Ennist designed one.

"That was an interesting thing to do because you have to get a lot of voltage into the circuit in a short span of time. We wound up buying second-hand transformers and very large capacitors that could withstand 2,000 volts across them. Once we put that together, we had to push this big switch to zap the circuit. It was kind of nerve-wracking pushing the switch knowing there was 2,000 volts there. Back then, it was cutting-edge to do that."[12]

The Next Generation

The two engineers next postulated they could use a microprocessor to make an accessory to the Key-Lux phone system. They created a "little black box" with a chip controller in it and an amplifier. The box allowed customers to tie together several phone lines and hold a conference call.

During the development, there was a lot the Inter-Tel team didn't know about working with a microprocessor, but Mihaylo trusted them to come up with solutions.

Their code, for instance, was painstakingly programmed and manually programmed into the memory chips. This was partially to save money, Peiffer remembered, and partially because they didn't know about development tools. The program itself was written on paper with the corresponding machine code written in the left margin. Once that process was completed, Peiffer sent the job to an outside vendor to program the memory.

With the conference call unit up and running, the microprocessor was proving itself admirably. Both test projects had been successful and the technology was within Inter-Tel's grasp. It was the next step that was the risky one: develop the next-generation phone system and base it on microprocessors. In doing so, Inter-Tel would meet its dealers' demands for a new product and be one of the first telecommunications companies to offer a microprocessor-controlled digital key telephone system.

Mihaylo left the project to Peiffer and Ennist while he concentrated on setting up yet more dealers and distributors. This pattern of delegation, of trusting employees with key elements of his business, was becoming a major strength in his management style. Not only was Mihaylo loyal, he generated great loyalty throughout his company.

The system the engineers worked on was critical. With the race on to develop digital telephone systems, this next-generation product was integral to Mihaylo's ambition of becoming a national player, and he wanted to make sure the distribution was in place. He also agreed to buy the team a $5,000 Motorola Exorciser, an early version of a personal computer that allowed Peiffer to type in code on a terminal and test run the program. "That was a big deal," Peiffer said.

"It was one of those things that you wished you had done sooner. It used an 8-inch floppy disk and from then

on, I thought I was in heaven developing code for micro-
processors. After you were done with your code, it would
copy the code into memory, and then you could move it
over to the system and it would actually start running."[13]

Mihaylo also suggested that Inter-Tel form a joint venture with Taiko. By bringing Taiko into the development, the resulting product could be moved into production quickly because of the Japanese engineers' familiarity with the project. The two companies had also developed a very strong relationship through the Key-Lux project, and Mihaylo was a frequent visitor to Japan. Taiko agreed to the project and sent two engineers to the United States to help Inter-Tel develop a full microprocessor system.

The Team

Mihaylo had high hopes for his new system. Before the work began, he showed Peiffer promotional brochures for the big AT&T and ROLM PBX systems and said, "Put as many of these features as you can inside our key telephone system and we'll sell them competitively to small customers. We can make a fortune if the microprocessor is as powerful as we think it is."[14]

There were a total of six people on the team. Ennist, Peiffer and the two Japanese engineers were joined by Michael Yu, an Inter-Tel hardware designer, and James Muchler, an engineering technician. To insulate them from the distractions of the office and give them working room, Mihaylo moved them to a separate facility. "He wanted us to be totally separated from the Key-Lux," Peiffer recalled. "This is going to be a major project. It's a joint venture. We want to get it done as quickly as possible."[15]

The team worked through 1978 and 1979 on the new system. For the engineers, it was exciting work because they were working on the cutting edge, out in front of everybody else, and the team came from different backgrounds. "It was real interesting because the Japanese basically knew no English," Ennist said.

> "But they were good engineers, and we could deal with them on that level. But just learning to associate with them and communicating was a challenge. Since we were locked away with them for such a long period of time, we got to know them real well. I'm sure there were times when we thought we were saying one thing, and something else happened, but yeah, it was good we got together with them. They gave us the expertise of some of their background, and we combined that with what we knew about American phone systems."[16]

The development also presented technical challenges. Microprocessors were still a new technology, and Inter-Tel was at the very outer edge of the technology curve. Nobody had gone before them to establish protocol or development tools, so the team simply thought their way around the corners of problems as things came up, according to Ennist.

> "Some of the new products were stuff none of us had really ever worked on. The microprocessors were just becoming available. One of my early assignments had to do with simulating microprocessor operation in the telephone. There were no tools to do that. In order to simulate that, we came up with a piece of hardware that was about a foot square and would act like a microprocessor in a telephone. We had all these wires connecting over to it, and the telephone itself was

clunky and had mechanical switches. But it was what we needed to get it to work. That was exciting to be doing that type of work because we felt there was no one else doing it."[17]

By 1980, the team had successfully developed a groundbreaking pair of prototype systems, nicknamed Norman and Norma. The SPK (for Stored Program Key) system was revolutionary for Inter-Tel in many ways. By incorporating microprocessors into the design, Inter-Tel offered the first microprocessor-controlled phone system for its market. The SPK brought features like a message center, recorded music for holding callers, three-way calling and toll restriction within the reach of thousands of small to medium businesses. All that remained was enthusiastic market acceptance.

Fueled by the huge success of the SPK-1, Inter-Tel broke ground to build a new headquarters in Chandler, Arizona. Steve Mihaylo is second from left.

CHAPTER EIGHT

RING...NO ANSWER

"We couldn't let our customers down."

— Steve Mihaylo[1]

INTER-TEL UNVEILED THE STORED PROGRAM KEY (SPK) telephone system in 1980. The small company was ahead of everybody with its new product. Giants like Nippon Electric and Mashusta (Panasonic), which both attempted to harness the power of the micro-processor, encountered endless obstacles and delays. Others, like Datapoint and TRW, abandoned their efforts altogether.[2] Even TIE/Communications, Inc., the same company that had trounced the Key-Lux with hands-free answer-back, was still two years away from manu-facturing a competitive product.[3]

The victory was made sweeter when the engineers discovered that Inter-Tel was the first company in the world to commercially utilize the Motorola 6801 micro-processor. "We beat GM with its design for the automo-tive ignition, and we became the first customer of

Motorola to use that design," Peiffer recalled.[4] It was quite an accomplishment for an engineering team that started with no experience in chip programming and managed to turn out a working product in just two years.

Unlike its electromechanical predecessors, the SPK allowed special features to be programmed into the system's database depending on the customer's needs. It was a customizable system with a capacity of 120 phones. With few competitors able to offer that kind of flexibility on comparably sized systems, SPK sales boomed amid glowing media reports, and Inter-Tel became the darling of the telecommunications industry. "The only competing product out there was one they called the AT&T Horizon Telephone System, which was about four times as expensive and didn't do hardly anything," recalled Peiffer.[5]

Bell's other product, the Comkey series, comprised the majority of key systems installed in the United States. The system design, however, was more than 30 years old, and it was considered one of the largest and most obsolete installed bases of telephone equipment in the nation. Of the 4.5 million keyset systems in North America, approximately 90 percent of the equipment was obsolete. The $20 billion market was wide open.[6]

Confidence surged throughout the company. As one visiting reporter for the *Phoenix Business Journal* wrote, "There is no mistaking a healthy, happy, robust feeling that permeates Inter-Tel's offices in subtle and not-so-subtle ways."[7] It looked as if Mihaylo's aspirations for Inter-Tel were finally coming to fruition. The national distribution network began pumping a steady stream of SPKs across the country. In 1980, Inter-Tel posted revenue of $10.3 million. The SPK would push sales past $40 million within the next year.

Driven by his first major product launch, Mihaylo was able to realize another long-running ambition. Ever since founding Inter-Tel, Mihaylo had wanted to take his company public. The prestigious underwriting firms of Bache Halsey Stuart (now Prudential Securities) and E.F. Hutton agreed to sponsor the company. The following year, Goldman-Sachs, the same company that financed General Motors, and EF Hutton did a second stock offering.

On February 5, 1981, common shares of Inter-Tel stock were offered at $12.50 per share.

The stock sold out within the first 30 minutes. By the time the last trade was made, it had reached $16. "In a couple of days it went from $16 to $19. It hung around $19 to $20 for a couple of weeks, broke through $20 and then had a run to $24. It consolidated its gain, made another run to $24. It consolidated its gain, made another run to $28 and consolidated its gain again, and then peaked at $54," explained George Hays, Inter-Tel's vice president of finance from 1981 to 1983.[8]

In 1981, Inter-Tel made its debut on *Inc. Magazine's* list of the 100 fastest-growing small businesses (the small-business equivalent of the *Fortune* 500 list). Mihaylo and his top managers were compared to overnight successes Stephen Wozniak and Steven Jobs at Apple. *The Phoenix Business Journal* touted how "an ordinary-looking telephone has made millions for a trio of Phoenix executives and has made their company one of the glamour stocks of the burgeoning electronics industry."[9]

Steve Sherman, now with the title of executive vice president, purchased 8 percent of the company for $100,000. Sherman was second only to Mihaylo himself in the company hierarchy. The night after the stock offering, Sherman was still in New York City, where he had been working with the underwriters. As it sunk in that he was worth millions, he took to the freeway in a sports car, hung his head out the window and belted out the lyrics, "I have the world on a string!" He later described the feeling: "Here

I am, a 30-year-old kid. Raised in Brooklyn. My father was an immigrant. Working with my best friend. I thought I was the Steve Jobs of Arizona."[10]

But no one benefitted from the offering as much as company founder Steve Mihaylo. At one point, Sherman joked that his friend was suddenly an aspiring "unitarian," with a "unit" being $100 million. Mihaylo's reward, however, could never change his trademark frugality. In the years before the offering, friends remember Mihaylo asking them to sign a guest log as they entered his home. He used the log to justify writing off the house as a business expense. After the offering, Mihaylo still drove his Buick Riviera, and his exhortations to save a few dollars on an airline ticket or hotel room became a friendly joke around the office. Some even suggested that was the chief reason he learned how to fly. "His biggest joy in life is getting airline tickets at the cheapest price,"[11] joked Karl Eller, one of Inter-Tel's first board members and a longtime friend.

He also pursued his passion for flight and invested in a company called OMAC (for "Old Man's Airplane Company") to design and manufacture airplanes. This endeavor was very dear to Mihaylo's heart. He invested more than $10 million of his own money in the project, and the company ultimately designed a working prototype. The plane received technical certification by the Federal Aviation Administration but was never certified for commercial use or sale. This, coupled with sudden and pressing demands at Inter-Tel, ultimately forced him to abandon the project.

The Good Times Roll

The success of the SPK landed Inter-Tel on *Today's Business* 1981 list of the five best-managed companies in

Arizona.[12] The publication hailed Inter-Tel as a future contender: "They know what they've got to do to make this a big company, and they're doing it. That says something for the dynamism of Inter-Tel."[13] Throughout the company, managers and Inter-Tel loyalists were rewarded with stock options, and the mood around the office was buoyant.

Mihaylo and Sherman stepped up their efforts to expand the company. Inter-Tel established a direct-sales office in St. Louis, Missouri, and acquired its first company, an interconnect distributor called TCI that served the Southern California market. TCI had long been one of Inter-Tel's most profitable customers, with sales of $12.4 million in 1981. The acquisition solidified the company's position in California. Shortly after the acquisition, Mihaylo asked Craig Rauchle, Inter-Tel's manager in Denver, to relocate and take over Inter-Tel's operations on the West Coast and clean up the operation. When he moved in, Rauchle remembers walking into a tense situation of employee unrest, turnover and customer dissatisfaction, but he soon made the business successful.

Inter-Tel also entered into a series of Original Equipment Manufacturing (OEM) agreements to market phone systems to wholesale distributors. Through these agreements, Inter-Tel designed and manufactured products for other terminal equipment suppliers, some of whom packaged and resold the systems and instruments under their own brand. Datapoint, North Supply and Honeywell Communication Services all signed on with the program.

Internally, Inter-Tel instituted an employee stock option and thrift retirement plan to attract experienced managers. In an industry that suffered a shortage of qualified engineers and managers, Mihaylo began recruiting from some of the industry's most prestigious companies. More than one individual came out of or delayed retirement to be part of the booming company.

Inter-Tel even hired George Hays, vice president of finance, away from E.F. Hutton in 1981.[14]

While Mihaylo actively recruited a number of top employees during this period, others came because of what they had heard about the company. Tom Parise, a young regional manager for Coca-Cola, read about Inter-Tel in the local paper and arranged an interview for a sales job. "I didn't think Coca-Cola was going to take me where I wanted to go," Parise recalled.

> *"I had started doing some research. I had read about divestitures and the imminent breakup of the Bell system. I thought it was interesting because I liked telephony. And I was always intrigued by the stock market. I thought maybe I'd be a stockbroker, and I interviewed for a couple of positions. But then I said, 'I don't think I really want to do this.' About that time, I started to notice a little bit about a company going public called Inter-Tel. There was this guy, Steve Mihaylo, who founded it and was running it, and I found it to be interesting, and it talked about the divestiture of AT&T, and it mentioned computerized telephone systems. I said, 'Wow! I like computers. I like telephones. I like pubic companies. I've got to get in on this deal somehow.'"[15]*

Parise saw an ad in the local paper that Inter-Tel was hiring sales reps and responded. To his dismay, he was turned away after his first interview. But Parise was unwilling to accept the rejection.

"My wife and I were on our honeymoon in Mexico," he remembered, "and I was really distraught about not getting this job. So I made a collect call from Mexico and got ahold of the vice president of sales and said, 'Hey, I can't believe you didn't give me the job.' He said, 'Are you really calling collect from Mexico?' I said, 'Well, I don't have

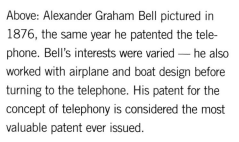

Above: Alexander Graham Bell pictured in 1876, the same year he patented the telephone. Bell's interests were varied — he also worked with airplane and boat design before turning to the telephone. His patent for the concept of telephony is considered the most valuable patent ever issued.

Above Right: Thomas Watson, pictured in 1874, was the mechanically minded machinist who helped Bell make the devices he imagined. Mr. Watson was the recipient of history's first phone call.

Right: Steve Mihaylo, pictured in the late 1960s, started his intercom sales business, Inter-Tel, the day after launch of the Apollo 11 moon mission, which landed the first men on the moon.

These ads touted the advantages of a private phone booth equipped with a Bell telephone. AT&T began as the long-distance unit of the American Bell Company. As a signal of how important long-distance service would be to the future of the telephone, it soon became the principal operating unit of Bell. Theodore N. Vail (below), shown talking on a "pencil phone," was brought into AT&T as the general manager in 1907. The organization he imposed on AT&T proved so successful it would remain intact until the federal government broke up AT&T in the 1980s.

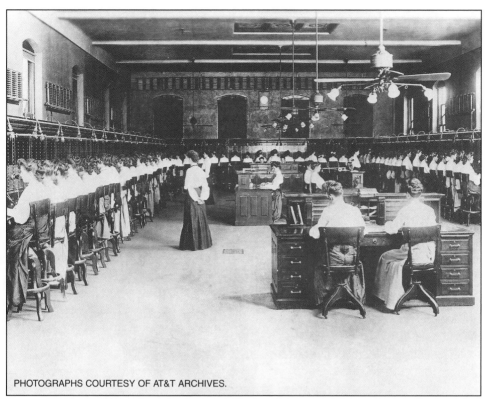

Above: From the very first, the telephone industry was driven by technological innovation. These women are switchboard operators in AT&T's main office in Kansas City, Missouri, in 1904.

Left: By 1926, the prosperous nation was in love with the telephone. This public telephone is in two parts, one mounted on the telephone pole and one sitting on the desk.

Left: The Bell System 70B1 "telephotography" apparatus was providing commercial fax service to the Associated Press in 1935. AT&T equipment was used to send and receive images as early as 1925.

Below: In 1938, the first AT&T No. 1 Crossbar was installed in Brooklyn, New York. Mechanical switching technology made it possible for the phone network to handle much more traffic.

Stevie

Above: Steve, shown at age four, was the second of Anne's five sons.

Left: Anne DeRitis and John Mihaylo pictured in 1936, the year the two met.

Below: The Mihaylo boys, shown in 1951 on New Year's Day, with their father. In descending order, there is Happy, Steve, Chuck, Matthew and Andy.

Above: Steve and the three younger Mihaylo boys, pictured at the Chrisman's home on Big Bear Lake in 1957. Andy, the youngest, moved back home with their mother after living at Auntie Knappen's while the others went into foster care. Mrs. Mihaylo, now divorced, couldn't support them by herself.

Left: After leaving the Marines, John Mihaylo joined the Los Angeles County Sheriff Department as a deputy.

ST. LUKE HOSPITAL

Above: Anne's 1958 graduating class. She had wanted to be a nurse since girlhood and put herself through the rigorous program. It was the realization of her life's dream. Anne is pictured in the back row, third from the left.

Left: Steve, shown to the right of Duska Bushelle, a family friend, with his three younger brothers. In 1959, Anne graduated as a nurse and was able to take her youngest boys back. Happy lived alone at this point.

Bottom Left: At Fort Ord, pictured with his stepmother Grace and brother Matt, Steve went to Mechanics School. At the same time, he also became an accomplished tailor and made money on the side tailoring uniforms for other men on base.

Above: Once out of the Army, Steve pulled a trailer with all his belongings to Phoenix and started a new life in the booming city. His first job was working for Western Electric.

Below: Steve Mihaylo, third from right, enjoys a meal with the Chester family in 1972. Mihaylo and Conway and Nancy Chester were originally partners in Inter-Tel.

Above: Early Inter-Tel staffers are shown at the 1976 North American Telecom Association Trade Show, one of the very first that Inter-Tel attended. From left to right are Tom Peiffer, Al Maynard, Steve Mihaylo and Steve Sherman.

Below: When Tom Peiffer joined Inter-Tel as its first engineer, he was committed to overhauling the Key-Lux. This early diagram shows some of the features Mihaylo wanted incorporated into the phone.

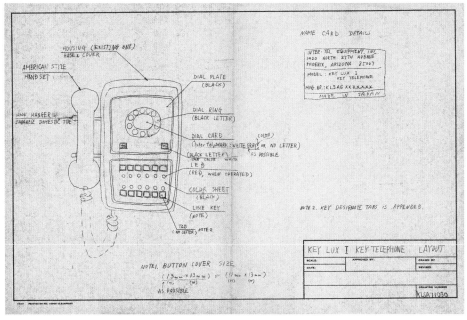

Above: Steve Mihaylo and Daisuke Higo, president of Taiko Electric Works, signing the first agreement between Inter-Tel and Taiko in Tokyo in 1973.

Below Left: The SPK-1 was the end result of Inter-Tel's foray into microprocessor-controlled phone systems. It was the first microprocessor-controlled system for its market and established Inter-Tel as a technological innovator.

Below Right: After proving microprocessors had potential, Peiffer bought a Motorola Exorciser, which allowed him to automatically program a Motorola 6801 microprocessor chip.

Top: Inter-Tel's new 154,000-square-foot headquarters at 6505 West Chandler Blvd. in Phoenix. This facility housed administration, warehousing, engineering, and research and development in the same building.

Center: U.S. Congressman, and future Senator, John McCain attended the new headquarter's ribbon cutting. From left are Steve's wife Lois Mihaylo, Cindy McCain, John McCain and Steve Mihaylo.

Right: Richard Long was hired as Inter-Tel's second president in 1982. He came in the middle of a crisis as the SPK phone system had major problems, and a series of high-level defections bruised Inter-Tel.

Above Left: After more than 30 years at GTE, Maurice Esperseth was hired as the head of engineering for Inter-Tel. He spearheaded the project to introduce the GX and GLX. (*Photo courtesy of Maurice H. Esperseth.*)

Above Center: While dean of the Engineering College at Arizona State University, C. Roland Haden helped establish the "ASU connection" and encouraged many top software students to work at Inter-Tel.

Above Right: Dr. Dave Pheanis, an ASU professor, was brought in as a consultant to help write code for the Galaxy. The code his team wrote would form the foundation of Inter-Tel technology for a decade. (*Photo courtesy of Dave Pheanis.*)

Middle Left: Jeff Ford started working part-time at Inter-Tel in 1983, fresh out of college. He was one of a group of recent software engineering graduates who would form the core research department at Inter-Tel.

Left: The GLX enabled small businesses to have a phone system with the same features that had been previously available only on big PBXs. It established Inter-Tel's position in the small- to mid-size business market.

Above: Ralph Marsh, on the far left, was hired to help manage acquisitions. At the same time, Tom Parise, right, was rapidly rising through the ranks of the young company. They are pictured with the new GMX phone.

Above Right: Duane Floyd, founder of Interconnect Communications Corporation, joined the Inter-Tel staff in 1987 when Inter-Tel bought out ICC.

Right: Jim Chumney was hired in 1985 and began working on the ESPDX phone system.

Below: After building Inter-Tel's engineering department, Maurice Esperseth, pictured to the right of Steve Mihaylo, retired in 1989, but remained on the company's board of directors.

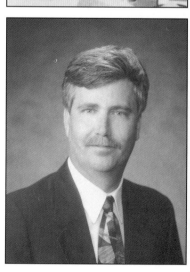

Above and Right: Inter-Tel signed an agreement with Premier Telecom to distribute the Premier ESP, which was based on the GX-120. It was the largest account at Inter-Tel, worth up to $25 million annually.

Right: In 1991, Mihaylo pitched in to help correct component problems in the GLX system.

Below Right: Chuck Oakley joined Inter-Tel during a spree of acquisitions. He had worked for a major distributor, TSI, in Texas.

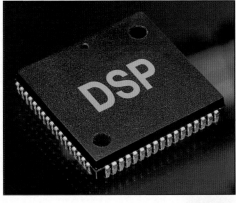

Above: In the early 1990s, Inter-Tel moved into its current design and distribution facility on Boston Street in Chandler, Arizona.

Left: Pictured in the Chandler building, from left, Tom Parise, Craig Rauchle, Steve Nichols, Steve Mihaylo and Ralph Marsh.

Left: Inter-Tel's answer for an all-digital product was the AXXESS telephone, which was introduced in late 1993. The AXXESS system used digital signal processors, an unheard-of development for a phone system.

Below Left and Right: The AXXESS phone was developed to function seamlessly in a modern office setting with local-area-networks (LAN) and computer telephone integration (CTI).

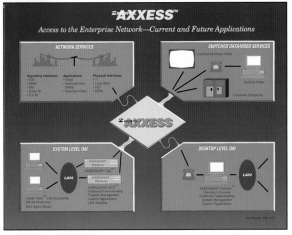

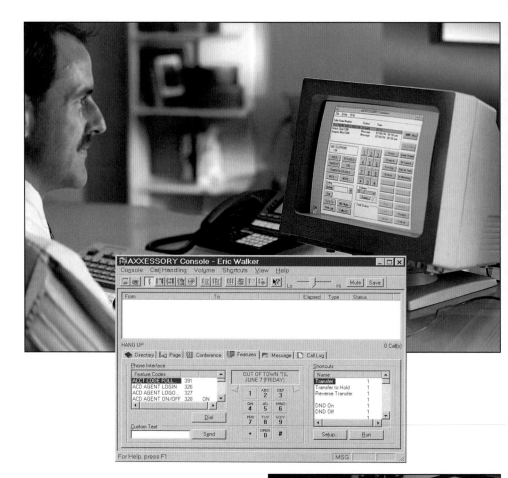

Above: The AXXESS computer telephone integration applications allow users to dial and talk using the power of the personal computer, as well as store data and retrieve customer files for call-handling efficiency.

Inset: The Features window of the AXXESSORY application provides users all the benefits of computer telephone integration.

Right: Pictured in 1996, the top three executives at Inter-Tel, from left, Steve Mihaylo, Craig Rauchle and Tom Parise, who retired in 1998 for personal reasons.

enough money for the call. I just want to let you know that if you don't hire me, when I get back there, I'm going to your major competitor and I'm going to sell against you until you do hire me.'"[16]

Parise found a job waiting for him upon his return.

Inter-Tel also purchased a new facility. Located in the Phoenix suburb of Chandler, the new $6 million, 154,000-square-foot manufacturing and administrative facility would take more than a year to be completely occupied. For the first time in the company's history, all administrative, warehousing, engineering, and research and development functions would be performed at a single location. In the meantime, Inter-Tel continued to occupy its building on 33rd Avenue in Phoenix.

The company also introduced the "little brother" to the SPK, a smaller version of the key-system called the MPK. The MPK offered many of the SPK's features but

Tom Parise, pictured in 1984, was turned down for a job after his first interview. He got the job and later became the third president of Inter-Tel.

had a capacity of 32 telephones compared to the SPK's 120 telephones. With the MPK, Inter-Tel hoped to tap into an unexploited corner of its market. The MPK product introduction was followed by a second stock offering in February 1982.

Unfortunately, the MPK's release and the second stock offering were overshadowed by a growing concern within the company. Shortly after the first SPKs were shipped, Inter-Tel began receiving complaints that the system was unreliable. To some extent, this is expected in any new, innovative product, especially one involving extensive software. But instead of going away, the trickle of calls had been steadily growing into a torrent. By late 1981, it was clear that Inter-Tel was in trouble. Customers were complaining that the SPK was a technical failure and wanted something done about it. Right away. The good times were about to end.

Ring ... No Answer

With thousands of systems already shipped, it was a bad time to learn the SPK was causing problems. Without warning, entire office systems crashed and lines went dead in mid-conversation. One of the most devastating complaints was that outside callers heard endless ringing, but the phone itself would never signal an incoming call. Business owners who relied on contact with the outside world were infuriated as they imagined frustrated customers not being able to get through and potential sales literally hanging up. Inside Inter-Tel, the phenomenon was coined "ring ... no answer."[17]

There were also complaints of background noise and sporadic call merging, where separate lines would suddenly connect and produce unwanted conference calling. Explained SPK engineer Bill Ennist: "The SPK was a time division system so that the channels were floating, and we had a lot of merging where you'd be on one call and you'd hear somebody else. Automatic conferencing that you weren't expecting. That was a major, major problem."[18]

As the complaints mounted, rumors of huge lawsuits began to circulate. Mihaylo recognized that something had to be done. In the early months of 1982, Steve Mihaylo and Steve Sherman approached Gerhardt Klaiber, who was in the process of consolidating telecommunications operations at the German electronics giant Seimens. The two described the problem at Inter-Tel and asked Klaiber if he could fix it. Calling it a "great adventure," Klaiber quit his job at Seimens, moved from Boca Raton, Florida, to Phoenix and "walked right into a hornet's nest."[19]

Klaiber, who was hired as a senior vice president, remembered his first visit to a client:

> "We were received in a customer's board room. The assembled chairman of the board, the president and various other executives were ready to shoot us. We were greeted with the threat of massive lawsuits for all kinds of damages that we had cost their company. I, having just stepped into the company, didn't know too many things. I just said, 'Look, here's where I come from. This is what I have done, and I am very familiar with virtually all aspects of this business. I can only promise you that I will fix it as fast as it is humanly possible to fix it.'"[20]

Terry Buffard also felt the heat of discontent over the SPK phone system. Buffard started working at Inter-Tel in 1980 in the repair department as a technician. Within less than a year, the SPK problems erupted, and he spent the next three harrowing years more "on the road than at home."

"Some of the customers that we'd walk into, those first 10 minutes were really bad. People would scream at you, and you'd hear every four-letter word about the product and how lousy the company was you worked for. Our job in tech support was to go out to all these customer sites that were having troubles and take new software with us. Sometimes we'd be waiting for software to be Fed-Exed to us. We were the eyes and the hands for engineering just to tell them what we were seeing."[21]

Mihaylo, who at various times in his life has described himself as "introverted" and "timid" and has been described by friends as "strong-willed," kept himself controlled throughout the entire SPK crisis. It wasn't the first time he had faced adversity, and he was prepared to do anything necessary to stand by his customers. Through his determination, he inspired confidence in his employees.

"The way we did damage control was by communicating with our customers, letting them know what we were doing to alleviate their problems. We concentrated on the ones that were ready to throw their systems out. Just communicating with them and begging. There was a lot of begging. We couldn't let our customers down. I think that was the bottom line, when you got to the point where they just had enough and couldn't take the begging anymore, you begged them to hang in there a little longer. Surprisingly, we had very few customers that bailed out on us."[22]

Steve Sherman's reaction was much more emotional. "I thought I was having a nervous breakdown," he remembered. "I walked out of the building. I found myself walking by the railroad tracks. I was so worried. But

Steve didn't sweat. Nothing bothered him. He had great inner strength and confidence. This is a man who walked through a storm of competitors many times larger."[23]

In 1983, Mihaylo approached board member Karl Eller and asked him to serve as chairman of the Inter-Tel board. Eller was a well-known Arizona businessman who had just sold his company, Combined Communications Corporation, to the Gannett Corporation. "I gave him moral support," Eller recalled. "He asked me financial questions or whatever he needed, and we were all pitching in to help out."[24]

Meanwhile, the engineering team was having trouble ridding the SPK of its bugs. At times, almost every employee at Inter-Tel was called upon to help with menial but time-consuming tasks like burning-in new circuit boards. People worked nights and weekends to fix the system, but problems seemed to follow on each other's heels — as soon as one was resolved, something

Karl Eller joined Inter-Tel's board of directors just prior to Inter-Tel's going public in 1980 and during the SPK crisis.

else would go wrong. Inter-Tel clearly didn't have the kind of programming experience it would take to fix the software, so Klaiber called on a friend named Ed Terminy.

Terminy and Klaiber had worked together at Seimens. By 1982, Terminy had been writing telecommunications software for eight years. He had written code for an Intel 8080 chip and developed a successful PBX called the ST192. He held the title of director of engineering when he quit Seimens in 1982 to found his own consulting company. With so few qualified engineers in the field, it was critical for Inter-Tel to enlist Terminy's help.

"I talked him into it," Klaiber said, "I mean, really talked him into doing it. He agreed to drop virtually everything else and take two or three of his best guys. He took on a contract to develop the communication software that was necessary for this equipment to operate properly."[25]

In August 1982, Terminy traveled to Phoenix to fix Inter-Tel's ailing SPK system. When he sat down with Klaiber and Mihaylo, Terminy was impressed with the company that Mihaylo had built from zero and the founder's eagerness to fix the SPK at all costs.

"They were losing calls and there were complaints. The system appeared to be unstable. Steve asked me to do whatever I had to do. He gave me carte blanche that included anything. He opened up his wallet and said whatever it takes, do it."[26]

Terminy recognized the problem immediately. He had already designed three telephone switches based on microprocessors and "had fallen off that cliff before." The first, and easiest, problem to fix was the system's tendency to crash. Terminy knew from experience that any large software program with millions of bytes of information, whether it is a telephone switch or a desktop operating system, will have flaws. Today, that's an accepted fact of life. Software designers build multiple safeguards into every program during development, and there are still bugs. In the late 1970s, however, very few people had experience writing software for telephone systems, and the Inter-Tel team operated on intuition, luck and experimentation.

As a result, the SPK lacked basic system protection. Every time there was a problem, no matter how minor, the whole system crashed and all calls were dropped. Working with Tom Peiffer and an Inter-Tel engineer named Chuck Kelly, Terminy fixed this by writing recovery logic for the software. Known as a "soft restart," this recovery logic instructed the telephone system to automatically reboot when the software operating system hit a glitch. All the in-process calls were saved. The difference was dramatic. Before recovery logic, a system hiccup would result in the entire system crashing and all the calls being disconnected. After the soft restart had been programmed in, such problems were invisible to the caller as the phone system saved their connection and automatically rebooted.

This gave the team breathing space to confront the more fundamental problems with the SPK. Unfortunately, it turned out that the problem with the software was the software itself, which Terminy disparagingly nicknamed "spaghetti code."

"They just threw it together without designing it," explained Jim Chumney, a former aerospace engineer who started with Inter-Tel near the end of the SPK crisis. "They added features to the software willy-nilly without any process control, without any testing. The story goes that Steve Mihaylo would walk by and say, 'Gosh, it would be neat to have this feature.' Well by the next day, the feature would be in there, and it would be shipping out with the product."[27]

Fixing the tangled code promised to be a time-consuming, arduous task. Mihaylo stayed on top of the project, remembered Terminy, but it was never his style to micromanage the engineers. As in earlier development projects, Mihaylo placed a great deal of trust in his development team. He was content to dictate features of the end product and let his engineers manage the development. This was also true of the growing distribution network. As Inter-Tel reached across the country, Mihaylo gradually released his hold and trusted crucial elements of his business to key people.

"I've always believed that you should give people the power to make change, to do things in an organization," Mihaylo later said. "It's amazing, when you unleash that power, what it will do."[28] In fact, the company slogan was "People, technology and telephones," emphasizing that Inter-Tel had been built on its people. Mihaylo was the kind of manager who became personally involved with his employees and, in turn, expected their uncompromising dedication but also trusted their expertise.

By late 1982, Inter-Tel was still in trouble, but it was becoming clear that the company could fight its way through the thicket of problems and survive. Yet Mihaylo was about to face the most personal aspect of the crisis. The problems with the SPK could be overcome by hard work and a cool head, but what was about to happen struck at Mihaylo's core instincts.

Vodavi

In the middle of 1982, Steve Mihaylo decided it would be a good idea to bring in seasoned outside management. His reasons were varied. The SPK problems had caused an internal crisis of confidence. Also, the company had just gone public and "I was still only thirtysomething," Mihaylo remembered. "All the guys on Wall Street said, 'You need somebody with more gray hair in here to run this business.'"[29]

That summer, Steve approached Richard Long and asked him if he would be interested in running Inter-Tel. Long had just the kind of industry experience and prestige that Mihaylo was looking for. Long managed a large interconnect company in Texas until 1975, when he became president of the North American Telephone Association (NATA). Three years later, Long and his wife moved to Washington, D.C., and he accepted a job as executive director of NATA. From that position, he represented independent interconnect suppliers in the battle that was raging over the Justice Department's antitrust case against AT&T.

> *"Steve, who was on the NATA board, approached me and said he wanted people with some operating experience, hands-on stuff. He flew my wife and me out to Phoenix and we talked. I looked at his operation and decided that it might be something I would have a lot of fun at."*[30]

Despite his wife's misgivings that Arizona "looked like a giant box of kitty litter," the couple moved from Washington, D.C., and Long arrived at work with the title of executive vice president. He remembered walking into a lion's den of trouble.

> *"There were some folks there that had come in at very high levels, and he was paying them an awful lot of money. They went about restructuring the company, I think, without consulting Steve. He kind of got caught in the updraft, and I think it was a little bit out of control. I would have to say that I got caught in*

between what Steve wanted to get done and what these people he had recently hired wanted to do."[31]

Unfortunately, the high-ranking people Long referred to weren't all new to Inter-Tel. Chief among them was Steve Mihaylo's longtime friend and second-in-command, Steve Sherman. Since the beginning of the SPK crisis, Sherman had become increasingly unhappy at Inter-Tel.

"This was the worst of the worst. We had just gone public. Orders had gotten canceled. I was so worried. It was all well-intentioned, but the problems were overwhelming. And then Steve went into all these other businesses, airplanes, retail hardware stores, etc. He was defocused. Meanwhile, we had ring, no answer, all over the place. We had systems all over the country that were crashing. So I wanted him to leave. That's what this is really about. I wanted him to stay home and let me run the business. You know, when I came out to the company, I was just there to make money. And that's what I did. Lots of it. Except somewhere along the way, I fell in love with it. I felt that I had built it. I felt it was my company and I wanted to run it."[32]

Ultimately, it wasn't Mihaylo who left. Only months after Long was hired, Steve Sherman abruptly quit Inter-Tel to found a competitor. And he didn't go alone. He poached several of Inter-Tel's top engineers, including Gerhardt Klaiber, Chuck Kelly and an Inter-Tel salesman named Kent Burgess. The company they founded, also located in Phoenix, was called Vodavi (for "voice, data, video") and planned to compete directly with Inter-Tel.

Sherman said he got the idea to defect while Mihaylo and he were in Korea. The two were in business working with Taiko when Inter-Tel began developing a relationship with Goldstar, a large company controlled by a wealthy family in Korea. Sherman, however, encouraged Mihaylo to work with Taiko instead of Goldstar — even as he was negotiating with Goldstar to start up his own business. "They put their hand on me," Sherman remembered. "They told me they would marry me for life."[33] It was their financial backing that enabled Sherman to found his own company.

When Sherman told Mihaylo what was happening, Steve Mihaylo didn't launch into an angry tirade against his vice president. According to Sherman, he simply said, "OK. Go." Then he sued. Mihaylo felt Sherman had violated his duty to Inter-Tel by approaching Goldstar, which was negotiating to become an Inter-Tel supplier. Worse yet, when he established contact with Goldstar, Sherman advised Mihaylo not to do business with the company.

The crux of the problem, however, wasn't legal. It had to do with the difference in the two men. To Sherman, it was purely a business decision to leave Inter-Tel and found a direct competitor. To Mihaylo, who had moved from California to Arizona to avoid competing with Conway Chester, it was purely personal. His company was his life, and it would have been unthinkable to betray his employer as he felt Sherman was doing.

The lawsuit was resolved, but the relationship never healed. In 1998, Sherman recounted their contact since he quit.

"This happened early in the business. The business was booming. There was plenty of room and plenty of opportunity. But he didn't see it like that. I must have sent him a dozen letters and a dozen telephone calls. Right after I left, when I would be walking in the street, he would just cross the street. If we were at a function together, he walked out. We spoke in 1996. I ran into him

at a trade show, and I went up to his booth. He spoke so
harshly to me in the middle of a floor with thousands of
people, I started to cry. He treated me less than dead.

"Then last year, I was in Chandler driving past a
piece of land that we owned together at one time, and
I couldn't stop thinking about it. I picked up the phone
and called him. He always answers his own phone.
We spoke for about an hour. It was fantastic. But it's
sad. I don't think it will ever be fixed."[34]

With Sherman and Klaiber gone, Mihaylo appointed
Long president and chief operating officer of Inter-Tel.
But the relationship between Long and Mihaylo was
beginning to sour. "I got caught flat-footed," Long said in
a 1998 interview. "It was devastating."[35]

"What needed to be done was the whole lot of
these guys needed to be fired. But what happened
was the leaders of the team went over and defected
and started Vodavi. And then they began to cherry-
pick Inter-Tel. We didn't know who was with us and
who was against us. In retrospect, I can see that I just
wasn't strong enough. I wasn't vocal enough."[36]

Long thought the best way out of the crisis was
through sales. He wanted to dump more product into the
market; Mihaylo, on the other hand, felt cutbacks were
in order. He was already worried that the large build-up
in SPK inventory had damaged Inter-Tel enough, and he
didn't want to see the company fail. The two argued the
point for nearly six months until Mihaylo reasserted his
leadership. He offered Long the choice of either cutting
Inter-Tel down to size or taking over the sales operation
in California. Long replied that he didn't want to move to
California and was unwilling to undertake the wrenching

task of layoffs. Mihaylo gave him a day to make a final decision, but Long already knew his answer. The next day, Long's tenure with Inter-Tel was over. Two years after becoming president and COO of Inter-Tel, Long moved back to Washington, D.C., to become chairman of NATA. Under the circumstances, the two men parted on friendly terms.

This left two vacancies. Mihaylo resumed the role of president and was once again in charge of his company. To take over in Los Angeles, Mihaylo turned to Craig Rauchle, who moved from Denver to California for his company.

The years had been brutal. Inter-Tel posted a $1.8 million loss in 1983 and a larger one in 1984. The company's star product had almost driven Inter-Tel out of business, and a series of high-level defections had bruised both the company and Mihaylo. A cartoon circulated around the office of an executive seated at a desk and four men carrying the desk. It was labeled, "Here comes the new VP."

Throughout these years, Mihaylo carried in his briefcase a quote from Calvin Coolidge. The words embodied the attitude that had taken Mihaylo this far and would put Inter-Tel's fractured spirit back together:

"Nothing in the world can take the place of persistence. Talent will not. Nothing is more common than the unsuccessful man with talent. Genius will not. Unrewarded genius is almost a proverb. Education alone will not. The world is full of educated derelicts. Persistence and determination alone are omnipotent."

The GX-120 was one of the first phone systems to offer a liquid-crystal
display message window on the unit. Its success revived Inter-Tel with
almost flawless code, it helped heal the fractured company.

CHAPTER ☎ NINE

THE ASU CONNECTION

*"I didn't know anything about telephony. And I
brought in all these people that didn't know about telephony either. We were computer people, but we all said,
'Well, how hard can this be? We can do it.'"*

— Dr. David Pheanis[1]

THROUGH THE TOUGHEST YEARS OF THE SPK
crisis, Inter-Tel's engineering department was
dominated by hardware specialists. What little experience there was in writing software was self-taught.
Although Inter-Tel had heralded a revolution in key-set
phone systems with the SPK, Steve Mihaylo would later
remark, "It's always the pioneers who get arrows in their
backs." By 1983, Inter-Tel's reputation in the marketplace was in shambles and the stock had fallen to less
than $5. To re-establish itself, Inter-Tel had to ensure that
its next phone system was completely solid. And that presented a problem.

As the microprocessor began its rapid transformation of industry, there was a sudden and burgeoning
demand for software engineers. In the telecommunications industry, any experienced telephony software design-

ers already worked for giant corporations like Seimens, AT&T or GTE. Attracting this kind of talent would be expensive, and Inter-Tel was in no position to bestow lavish salaries on anybody.

After Richard Long left, Mihaylo streamlined his company: From 1983 to 1984, staff levels were reduced from 480 to 260. In the 30-year history of Inter-Tel, this is the only time the company has downsized. Mihaylo later described it as "the worst thing I've ever had to do in my entire business life."[2] Confirming his hawkish instincts on cost control, Mihaylo knew Inter-Tel was suffering from too many people and not enough customers. It was the classic formula for a loss and one that Mihaylo promised himself would never be repeated. Grimly, the company suffered through a series of "black Fridays."

Robert Craft, who served on Inter-Tel's board throughout the SPK crisis, remarked that Mihaylo "was reluctant to fire people. He was dedicated and very, very loyal."[3] In fact, the downsizing took a very personal toll on the company founder, who had built his company on a web of loyalty, to both customers and employees. That holiday season, when Inter-Tel traditionally distributed turkeys, it seemed a frivolous waste of money to spend the $35 or so on 500 turkeys. But Mihaylo, who in so many other cases was famous for thriftiness, insisted that the annual turkey giveaway would go ahead as usual.

At the time of the downsizing, Tina Sargent was Steve Mihaylo's secretary and saw first-hand the kind of suffering the downsizing caused her boss. Sargent had started with the company in 1981 and acted as an executive assistant to many of the company's top executives before being tapped to work as the CEO's secretary. "He had kind of a reputation for chewing up the secretaries and spitting them out," Sargent remembered in a 1998 interview, remarking that she cried when she found out she was to be his secretary.

"He was a very, very different person in those days than he is today. He was very, very intense and stressed out when we had to downsize. I think that one of the things that added to his stress level is that he chose to keep a handle on everything himself."[4]

Engineering Solutions

Even as the sales and operational staffs were reduced, Inter-Tel sought qualified engineers to design its new phone system, a problem it shared with many other high-tech companies. GTE Automatic Electric, the manufacturer of the industry's first digital PBX, was also having trouble keeping engineers. Although it was an established company where a talented engineer could make a comfortable living, GTE had a voracious appetite for software designers. In the early 1980s, the company tried to maintain a staff of 600 to 800 engineers but faced an annual turnover that ran as high as 25 percent.

In looking for a solution, GTE realized its efforts were hindered by geography. The huge electronics company was headquartered in Connecticut and had a large research and design facility in Chicago near O'Hare International Airport. Engineers who were hired from warmer climates like Texas and California moved north, worked for a year or two, then returned to the mild climes from which they had migrated. The company decided it was time to take corrective action. In 1978, GTE opened a multimillion-dollar research and development lab in Phoenix and put it under the charge of a 31-year GTE veteran named Maurice Esperseth.

While living in Phoenix, Esperseth became involved in a range of civic activities, including the local Chamber of Commerce, United Way and Junior Achievement. Steve Mihaylo was also active in Junior Achievement, and the two struck up a friendship. Meanwhile, Esperseth was becoming disenchanted at work. After 33 years of developing telecommunications systems for GTE, he was tired of the bureaucracy and was considering early retirement. When he mentioned this to Mihaylo over dinner one night, Mihaylo promptly offered him a job. Esperseth was interested. In 1983 he left GTE and was named the new head of research and development at Inter-Tel.

> *"For me, what it meant was a very exciting time because I was leaving a very large company with billions of dollars of sales. But GTE was very bureaucratic. To get a decision made, you had to go from Phoenix to Chicago to Stamford, Connecticut. I moved from that to Inter-Tel, which was fairly small. The executive staff was all within 30 feet of each other, so you only had to go 30 feet to get a decision made."[5]*

His first job at Inter-Tel was to gain control of the engineering department and begin designing a new phone system. "When I came here, the systems were so full of problems that every time they shipped one out the door, one of the vice presidents of sales said, 'Well, there goes another big problem,'" recalled Esperseth. "Steve and I talked about it, and based on my experience and what I'd been through, we decided to take a different approach. Rather than throw money at the problem, we would hire quality people. That, of course, brought up recruiting problems."[6]

Esperseth turned to Dr. C. Roland Haden, the dean of Arizona State University's College of Engineering, for advice. Before he started at Inter-Tel, Esperseth had been involved in fund raising for ASU and had become friends with Haden. When he described the situation, Haden suggested that Esperseth contact David Pheanis, a professor in the College of Engineering. Pheanis had just finished a consulting project for Sperry Flight Systems when Esperseth called him. "Maury called me out of the blue," Pheanis remembered. "I'd never heard of Inter-Tel. I came over and talked to Maury and reviewed the situation. He said, 'Well, can you do something to help?'"[7]

It didn't take long for Pheanis to conclude that the SPK's problems were insurmountable. The software was a hodgepodge of code precariously balanced to keep the system running. As had already been discovered, any changes crashed the system and introduced a new set of problems. "You could tell right away that there was no structure to the software," recalled Pheanis in a 1997 interview.

> *"I remember one thing that I still use as an example for my students. There was a series of about 15 pages of code with no comments. It was just instructions like 'Load A with count, increment A, decrement A,' stuff like that. This went on for 15 pages with not a single comment explaining why anything was being done. Right in the middle of this 15 pages, there was one instruction that had a comment. It said, 'test flag.' Very helpful. The only thing we could do with the software is pretend it wasn't there and start over."[8]*

Pheanis also identified the second major problem: the lack of software expertise at Inter-Tel. "I said, 'I can't fix it alone, and I don't think I can do it with your people because I don't think they'll be amenable to the kind of ideas of what it takes to do it right,'" Pheanis remembered.[9] Instead, Pheanis wanted to assemble a team of his own choosing. His proposition would cost, but since he planned on using former students, who were trained in software and computers, it would be less expensive than hiring experienced telephony engineers.

"I didn't know anything about telephony," remarked Pheanis. "And I brought in all these people that didn't know anything about telephony either. We were computer people, but we all said, 'Well, how hard can this be? We can do it.' That was a struggle at first because, of course, the people that were already in Inter-Tel were deeply into telephony, and they knew it, and they didn't think we would be able to do anything. They would snow us with buzz words, and we'd believe they knew what they were talking about, and then we'd realize afterwards, 'Oh, wait a minute. They don't really know.' Since then I've always said, if you ever have a choice between talent and experience, choose talent. They can develop experience. They can't develop talent."[10]

Pheanis' team ultimately consisted of 18 handpicked engineers, of whom 17 had studied at Arizona State University. Although few had professional experience, they were among the most outstanding students to graduate from one of the nation's top engineering colleges. In addition, since they all had the same background, Pheanis knew their methodologies would be consistent.

"We intentionally sacrificed the idea that a group of people from different backgrounds will generate fresh ideas, and we expected that we could get better ideas by hiring compatible people who had demonstrated they were at the top of their peer group," he explained.[11]

Louis "Skip" Welch was the first of Pheanis' recruits. When he was approached by Pheanis, he had been at Sperry Flight Systems, which later became Honeywell, for four years and had cultivated a dislike for the bureaucracy of a large company. When Pheanis offered him a chance to help build an engineering department from the ground up, Welch signed on — even though the most exposure he'd had to telephones was "picking them up and using them."

As he soon discovered, the new engineers had more to overcome than their own inexperience. The existing engineering staff resented their presence, and the Product Management Group (PMG) felt the new engineers were wasting company resources in redesigning the SPK. What the PMG really wanted was a product for the lucrative PBX market. Therefore, when it came time to specify the features for the new system, the PMG assembled a list of PBX functions. Welch remembered the situation:

"The Product Management Group specified the functionality of this new phone system, and they had picked and chosen from a number of different competitors, and a lot of them were big PBX features that were never put into a key-system-size phone system. We joked about it because there were some people in the Product Management Group that really felt that Inter-Tel shouldn't be designing a facelift to the SPK, but instead should be designing a PBX, and they put a list of features together that they thought maybe would choke the world."[12]

Despite their inexperience, or perhaps because of it, the new engineering team accepted the challenge. For the next 18 months, the group worked on the design and development of Inter-Tel's second microprocessor-controlled key system, which would be called the GX-120, or Galaxy. Because Inter-Tel was still building its Chandler headquarters, the engineering department worked in its own building and was buffered from the rest of the company.

Jeff Ford, another Pheanis recruit, started working for Inter-Tel while he was in his senior year at ASU. After graduating in 1984, he started as a software engineer and was on the GX-120 development team. "The entire engineering department was made up of brand-new graduates from ASU," he remembered. "The work environment was excellent."[13]

This group of young software experts represented the future of Inter-Tel technology. With the software-driven GX-120, the company had begun a migration away from hardware into software development. In time, Inter-Tel would specify that incoming engineers had to be degreed software engineers.

As the new engineers came into the company, a natural attrition took place. Many of Inter-Tel's veteran hardware engineers were uncomfortable in the new environment and left the company, although loyal Inter-Tel originals Tom Peiffer and Bill Ennist elected to stay. Within two years, more than 90 percent of the engineering department were ASU alumni. Inter-Tel continued to recruit Arizona State University's top engineering students for the next 15 years, skimming off the top two or three students every year. In fact, after his tenure with Inter-Tel ended, Esperseth considered the "ASU connection" his greatest contribution. "There's no substitute for having good quality people, especially in this very difficult area of writing software," he remarked.[14]

The MAP

Comfortable that his engineering team was in control, Mihaylo turned his attention to expanding the sales network. By this time, Tom Parise, the young manager from Coca-Cola, had made a name for himself and become actively involved in expanding the company's distribution network. "As we started to move to a software company, we also started to look at how distribution worked for us," Parise said. "What was the quickest, most cost-effective way to get to market? We realized that the distribution model that worked to get us to where we were wasn't going to work for the next level."[15]

Mihaylo had long believed in an almost even balance of direct-sales offices and dealers and stepped up his efforts to open Inter-Tel branches. By 1984, the company had established more than 13 direct offices, including sales offices in San Diego, Phoenix, Los Angeles, Orange County, Tucson, Denver, St. Louis and New Jersey. Some of these had been started from the ground up; others were established as the result of an acquisition. The distribution network included 150 dealers in the United States and Canada.

Although the company had reported losses for the previous two years, Inter-Tel revenues reflected a generally upward climb. This kind of financial power allowed Mihaylo to take advantage of acquisitions, another expansion tool that represented a practical way to add proven sales networks. Matthew Mihaylo, a CPA and one of Steve's younger brothers, started working for Inter-Tel in late 1982 and helped design the acquisition program. The Model Acquisition Program (MAP) was a four-step system designed to ease a distributor into Inter-Tel's family of direct offices.

In the first phase, Inter-Tel made an equity investment in the dealership to be acquired. Next, the company and the dealership entered into a two-year partnership. The third phase constituted the actual merger as Inter-Tel acquired all of the outstanding stock through an exchange. The fourth phase amounted to a post-merger operating period during which the dealership management turned the business into an Inter-Tel branch. The MAP program was first put to use in 1984, when Inter-Tel purchased The Communicators, a dealer based in the Dallas/Fort Worth area. For that acquisition, Craig Rauchle was named to The Communicators board of directors to help smooth the acquisition toward its conclusion. Later that same year, Matthew Mihaylo left Inter-Tel.

Since acquisitions promised to figure prominently in Inter-Tel's future, Steve Mihaylo began searching for a new controller to represent his company — the previous one left for Vodavi. It wasn't long before Ralph Marsh responded to his advertisement. Marsh, already in his late 50s, had taken early retirement from the national accounting firm of Touche Ross in Alaska and resettled in Arizona. By the time he saw Mihaylo's classified ad, however, he had become restless in retirement and was looking for some challenging work — even if he was overqualified for the position.

> *"I saw an ad that said they'd like to have a controller who could grow to be a chief financial officer. So I wrote him and said, 'Why don't you take a CFO who's wanting to be a controller for a while?' I was impressed with the fact that here was a company that had reported big write-downs in the prior two years and yet had a marvelous balance sheet. Very, very strong balance sheet, and I said to myself, 'This guy knows how to weather a storm.'"[16]*

Marsh would guide Inter-Tel through its largest acquisitions for the next eight years. His presence at Inter-Tel was fortuitous and well-timed. Competition in telecommunications had always been ferocious, but 1984 will always be remembered as the year the Justice Department finally prevailed over AT&T, and its 22 local operating companies were broken into seven regional companies, Bell Labs, a manufacturing division and a long-distance unit. The AT&T breakup touched off a frenzy of mergers and acquisitions and forever changed the American telecommunications industry by opening up huge new markets.

Writing of the breakup's impact, a reporter for *Fortune* magazine explained: "As the giant company proceeds to restructure itself and decide which markets it wants to emphasize, which to de-emphasize, smaller rivals are moving quickly into markets once beyond them. Their challenge is to get big enough fast enough to assure their long-term success before AT&T can respond. This race against time is the reason behind a good many of the acquisitions and joint ventures in telecommunication of late."[17]

AT&T's divestiture also generated rampant price cutting as companies slashed prices on their products to gain market share. For Inter-Tel, the price wars brought huge markdowns in inventory and added to its losses. Searching for a way to reduce manufacturing costs, Mihaylo secured a multimillion-dollar manufacturing agreement with Samsung Semiconductor and Telecommunications Corporation LTD of Seoul, Korea. The agreement included the manufacture of several of Inter-Tel's systems, the distribution of several of Samsung's products and provisions for joint venture.

The new agreement not only reduced manufacturing costs, but ended a souring relationship with Taiko. Inter-Tel finally brought a $100 million suit against the manufacturer in June 1986, the second lawsuit in the company's history. (The first was against Vodavi.) The complaint charged that Taiko "provided defective equipment, charged too much, delivered it too late, and hid information from Inter-Tel during contract negotiations."[18] Although the two companies would settle out of court, the lawsuit marked the end of a 15-year relationship.

Despite the success of companies like Inter-Tel, AT&T was the Goliath of the telephone industry. Before its 1984 breakup, the company boasted assets greater than Mobil Oil and General Motors combined. Its breakup was a monumental moment in American industry. (Logo courtesy of AT&T Archives.)

CHAPTER TEN

DEREGULATION

*"If you think the breakup of AT&T means opportuni-
ty for telephone equipment makers, think again. The
market is already overcrowded. ... The current leaders
aren't sitting content. They are attacking each other's
markets and price-cutting like mad. Their goal is to gain
as much market share as possible now before the AT&T
subsidiaries, Western Electric and/or the new American
Bell get their acts together and devise strategies to protect and increase their remaining market share."*

— *Forbes* reporter Jean Briggs[1]

THE AT&T BREAKUP THAT HAD SUCH A PRO-
found impact on the telecommunications industry
was a long time coming. The Justice Department
first brought suit against the phone giant in the 1940s,
but nothing substantial would begin happening until 30
years later, when the movement against the world's biggest
company began to pick up momentum.

For AT&T, the shift in attitude was an astounding development. AT&T viewed itself as the dignitary of the telecommunications industry and took its custody of the telephone
system seriously. Company executives frequently sounded
phrases like "social purpose" and "public interest," and the
company seemed genuinely concerned with and rightfully
proud of building one of the world's most efficient utilities.[2]
The problem, as AT&T saw it, was a handful of government
officials who were prejudiced against the company

simply because of its size. AT&T urged that if those officials could overlook their preconceptions, they would see AT&T's monopoly was in the nation's best interests.

Throughout the early 1970s, AT&T was guided by Chairman John deButts. A company man for close to 30 years, deButts embodied the Bell spirit. Describing deButts, telecommunications historian Steve Coll wrote, "He exuded leadership, power and privilege. He was a self-styled captain of industry, dressing in dark, conservative suits, flashing the obligatory gold cufflinks and watch. When he met a man, he shook his hand firmly and looked him in the eye; when he spoke, deButts' Southern drawl carried the authority of a general's wartime orders."[3]

When deButts took AT&T's helm in February 1972, sentiments were already swinging against the company. A number of government officials felt AT&T's motives were not in the public's best interest but were motivated by self-preservation. They argued that AT&T's monopoly was discouraging technology and that the public would be served better through competition. Looking to weaken the antitrust movement, deButts addressed the National Association of Regulatory Commissioners on September 20, 1973. In his speech to an audience of nearly 1,000 state utility regulators, reporters and AT&T executives, deButts argued persuasively:

> *"The time has come for a thinking-through of the future of telecommunications in this country, a thinking-through sufficiently objective as to at least admit the possibility that there may be sectors of our economy — and telecommunications [is] one of them — where the nation is better served by modes of cooperation than by modes of competition, by working together rather than by working at odds."*[4]

He received a standing ovation from the crowd of regulators, signaling that not everyone was opposed to AT&T's monopoly. The Commerce Department and the Department of Defense, for example, publicly defended AT&T's monopoly. Endorsing AT&T, the Commerce Department pointed out AT&T was a key player in the international industrial arena, and the Department of Defense argued that a reliable national telephone system was crucial to national security. In large part, AT&T still enjoyed the support of the government.[5]

The Suit

One man who disagreed, however, was Bernie Strassburg, bureau chief of the Federal Communications Commission. Strassburg was a dedicated trust-buster, and it was under his ten-year reign as bureau chief that the FCC handed down the 1968 Carterfone decision and pushed for the approval of MCI's 1970s private line application, which allowed the first long distance telephone service alternative to AT&T.[6]

Unfortunately for AT&T, its position at the FCC went from bad to worse after Strassburg retired. The new FCC chief, Walter Hinchman, was even more pro-competition. Hinchman "was highly suspicious of AT&T. He was more hostile to the phone company than even Strassburg had been during his last months on the job."[7]

AT&T complicated its position, and angered the FCC, by refusing to acknowledge the changing industry. In many ways, the company felt cheated. AT&T executives argued that the company had built and maintained the nation's telecommunications system, and competitors like MCI President Bill McGowan and equipment suppliers like Mihaylo were "cream-skimmers" looking for a free ride.

AT&T, however, was not content to sit back and complain. The company was repeatedly accused of monopolistic business practices in violation of FCC rulings, including attempts to block interconnection of terminal equipment. (Steve Mihaylo himself had encountered this when he installed his first telephone system in Frank Lewis' office and had trouble getting the lines switched.) To AT&T's competition, the company unquestionably crossed the line, yet as former ICA President James Sobczak remarked, "Despite AT&T's actions, the company didn't think it was doing anything wrong at the time."[8]

AT&T's support in Washington dwindled through the early 1970s amid charges of strong-arm business practices. By 1974, a number of antitrust suits had been brought against AT&T, including the high-profile suit by MCI President Bill McGowan. As W. Brooke Tunstall, AT&T's corporate vice president of organization and management systems, pointed out in his 1985 book *Disconnecting Parties*, "With scores of lawsuits in various stages underway throughout the decade, the Bell system was quite literally under siege by litigation."[9]

On November 20, 1974, U.S. Attorney General William Saxbe greatly magnified the situation when he brought an antitrust suit against the company on behalf of the Justice Department. Saxbe, finally fed up with the charges of monopoly, accused the Bell system of monopolizing telecommunications, forcing competition from the market and unlawfully favoring Western Electric products.

AT&T acted puzzled by the Justice Department's suit and argued the company was a regulated utility and exempt from antitrust laws. Explaining AT&T's position, Tunstall wrote, "The basis of antitrust theory is the assumption that monopoly is intolerable; but regulatory theory calls for a common carrier to operate as a monopoly with public oversight. ... AT&T argued that the

Department of Justice's suit placed the company in an impossible double bind. It objected to being punished by antitrust litigation for complying faithfully with its regulatory charter."[10]

The Bell Bill

Under attack, deButts hoped to defeat the antitrust case by pushing legislation through Congress that would legally grant AT&T monopoly status. This legislation, called the 1976 Consumer Communications Reform Act, or the Bell Bill, would award AT&T a legal monopoly in long distance service and the telephone equipment market.

AT&T argued that competition would necessitate a 75 percent rate increase to meet the direct costs of providing service.[11] Strassburg, the FCC bureau chief, explained the proposed legislation, saying, "They seek to curtail competition in terminal equipment on the grounds that rental revenue lost to the competitors will no longer be available to subsidize basic local telephone service."[12]

While still in debate in Congress, the Bell Bill had a paralyzing effect on AT&T's competition. As long as the bill stood a chance of passing, many telecommunication equipment manufacturers were unwilling to invest heavily in product development.[13] From a business standpoint, AT&T's stance was understandable. The terminal equipment market had become the plum of the telecommunications industry, with total shipments estimated at $250 million and growing. Independent telecommunications vendors like Inter-Tel had captured 25 percent to 28 percent of the market.[14] Furthermore, AT&T had more to lose than a few sales. In order to remain competitive, the company would have to replace many of its outdated PBXs with new equipment — an indication that perhaps AT&T was stifling competition. As *Business Week* pointed out in an article titled "The New New Telephone Industry":

> *"For the American Telephone & Telegraph Company and other phone utilities, the new competitive era is a mixed bag of hazards and opportunities. The new technology, uncontrollable in a competitive market, threatens premature obsolescence for a large part of the $120 billion worth of installed phones, wires and switching equipment."*[15]

AT&T also continued to argue that interconnect equipment could damage its network, leading the FCC to establish a federally run equipment certification program. The new registration requirements required that all terminal equipment meet certain standards and be registered with the FCC. This had an immediate effect on Inter-Tel, which in 1977 hired Bill Ennist, the company's second engineer, to wade through the thicket of regulations.

With the Bell Bill, however, deButts had asked for too much. He not only wanted MCI blocked from competing in long-distance service, but he had asked Congress to turn back the Carterfone decision and eliminate the interconnect industry altogether.

In the ensuing congressional hearings, Steve Mihaylo joined with Bill McGowan, the legendary chief of rebel start-up MCI, to testify about AT&T's abuses. Congressional lawyers later stated that "if deButts had not chosen to include phone equipment in the Bell Bill, and if AT&T had not resorted to strong-arm lobbying tactics, there was a solid chance in 1976 that Congress would have taken action to control long-distance competition by MCI."[16] As it was, the Bell Bill didn't stand a chance and never made it through Congress.

The Trial

With the Bell Bill dead, deButts resorted to stall tactics until he left the company in 1979. His approach ended with the appointment of a new chairman at AT&T. Whereas deButts was in no hurry to go to court, Charles "Charlie" Brown was eager to finish the suit. While mired in litigation, AT&T had helplessly watched as MCI grew to a multibillion-dollar company and equipment manufacturers gobbled up market share. For Brown, it was time to move forward.[17]

The antitrust suit went to trial in March 1981. In the months that followed, the Department of Justice's lead attorney, Gerald Connell, presented evidence that revealed a pattern of anti-competitive behavior on AT&T's part. Witnesses included the owners and executives of telephone equipment companies from across the country, many of whom had gone bankrupt. They described how Bell operating companies wouldn't buy their products because of Western Electric. They told of how long it took AT&T to furnish them with the protective couplers that were required. And they estimated how much AT&T's anti-competitive prices had cost them. All in all, they portrayed AT&T as a spoiled monarch rebelling against the FCC.[18]

In his cross-examinations, AT&T attorney George L. Saunders, Jr., adroitly defended the company. He depicted AT&T as a company trying to adapt to change while serving the best interests of its shareholders and the public. AT&T, he argued, was merely trying to adhere to confusing and sometimes contradictory regulations.

Not only was Saunders a talented lawyer, but he wholeheartedly believed in AT&T's defense. He saw the antitrust case as a "rip-off" and an "outrage." According to historian Coll: "Saunders believed passionately that AT&T was being victimized by greedy opportunists such as Bill McGowan, who used politics and the regulatory system to skim AT&T's profits, and by overeager government attorneys, who Saunders believed were carrying out a personal and political vendetta against the phone company simply because it was so large."[19]

As the trial progressed, the Justice Department and AT&T began negotiations outside the courtroom. Brown's eagerness to wrap up the case contributed to his willingness to consider a settlement — even one that might lead to divestiture of the operating companies. What he wanted in exchange was to lift the restriction contained in the 1956 consent decree that prohibited AT&T from entering the lucrative computer communications market.

The consent decree was a settlement born of the first antitrust case against AT&T. The 1949 suit, which sought to divest AT&T of Western Electric, also accused AT&T of anti-competitive actions; specifically that Bell's operating companies bought equipment only from Western Electric, which gave AT&T a captive monopoly in the phone equipment business.

In 1956 the suit ended somewhat abruptly. In exchange for being allowed to keep Western Electric, AT&T agreed not to enter the computer business. At the time it was a modest concession for AT&T; computers were still in their infancy, and AT&T didn't see much of a future in the technology. The settlement was a clear victory for AT&T, and at the time it outraged both the public and Congress.[20] As technology evolved, however, AT&T found the consent decree to be a bigger trade-off than was originally intended. The line between computer and communications technologies blurred, and AT&T found itself barred from a rapidly growing segment of the market.

While Brown and the Justice Department continued to negotiate, AT&T's hope of winning the antitrust case was diminishing. By late 1981, it looked as if the Justice Department might win. Brown recognized that his company stood little chance in open court.

Settlement

On January 8, 1982, 10 months after the trial started, AT&T and the Justice Department announced a settlement. The landmark agreement dismantled AT&T's national network and broke the company's financial and management structure into eight discrete corporations. AT&T would continue to own Western Electric and Bell Laboratories and provide long-distance services, but the 22 Bell operating companies would be broken into seven independent companies, each serving a geographical region.[21] The settlement also lifted the restrictions prohibiting AT&T from computer communications, which represented the company's only victory in an agreement that cost two-thirds of its assets.

In a press conference following the settlement agreement, AT&T Chairman Charlie Brown announced, "Today's action disposed of a matter of importance to the AT&T company. It gets rid of restrictions that are contained in the 1956 consent decree. No one contemplated 25 years ago that a revolution in modern technology would largely erase the difference between computers and communications. As a consequence, the Bell System has been effectively prohibited from using the fruits of its own technology. And this new decree will wipe out those restrictions completely."[22]

The confusion and chaos that accompanied the reorganization of the nation's telephone system left many questioning if breaking up AT&T had been the right decision. In a retrospective for *Telecommunications* magazine, Tunstall wrote:

"Divestiture's first impact on 90 million businesses and residential customers was extreme confusion. Within a month, The Wall Street Journal *headlines read: 'AT&T's Split Proves Frustrating to Homes, Businesses Across US.' Two of the most serious complaints were that customers did not know whom to call for installation, repair or assistance and when they did call, the Bell companies blamed AT&T and AT&T blamed the Bell companies; and that receiving two bills from two companies in one envelope each month was confounding, particularly since many were error-ridden due to the complexity of the changeover."*[23]

For Inter-Tel, the most crucial part of the decision had to do with equipment manufacturing — and it represented both good and bad news. The newly independent operating companies were permitted to sell terminal equipment but not allowed to manufacture it. Huge markets opened up as the operating companies were free to buy products from the most competitive supplier.[24]

Equipment manufacturers began beating a path to the newly formed operating companies' doors, and a new wave of competitors entered the market. Unfortunately, the market was already oversaturated. As *Forbes* reporter Jean Briggs put it, "If you think the breakup of AT&T means opportunity for telephone equipment makers, think again. The market is already overcrowded. ... The current leaders aren't sitting content. They are attacking each other's markets and price-cutting like mad. Their goal is to gain as much market share as possible now before the AT&T subsidiaries, Western Electric and/or the new American Bell get their acts together and devise strategies to protect and increase their remaining market share."[25]

While the divestiture opened up new markets, it also caused a sudden increase in competitive pressure that contributed to Inter-Tel's losses of the mid-1980s. The competition also had another far-reaching effect: it caused the pace of innovation to accelerate rapidly. Market share was critical to success, and one sure way to increase market share was to have the most technologically innovative product.

Inter-Tel's answer to this need lay with a group of young engineers putting the final touches on its new phone system.

Through an OEM agreement with Premier Telecom Products, Inc., Inter-Tel produced the Premier ESP, a highly successful derivative of the Galaxy system.

CHAPTER ELEVEN

GALAXY

"The strength that evolved from the GX built our reputation back as a company. GX got us the credibility in terms of the dealers and the end-user customers, and then the ESP really propelled us back into the spotlight."

— Craig Rauchle[1]

INTER-TEL UNVEILED ITS NEXT-GENERATION PHONE system in 1985. The engineering department, aware that Inter-Tel's reputation was riding on it, had worked for almost two years rewriting code. The result of the effort was the GX-120 — also called the Galaxy — family of keyset phone systems. "It took longer than we estimated," said Maury Esperseth. "We had hired computer people. It turned out to be easier for these young, bright people to learn the telephone business than to teach the computer business to old-time telephone people. But they were new to it, and Steve Mihaylo was very patient."[2]

Unfortunately, the GX-120 was not an especially well-timed release. After AT&T was dismantled, the market had been quickly saturated with keyset telephones, and a wave of mergers swept through the industry.

Competitors all around Inter-Tel began reporting huge losses as profit margins almost vanished.

What the Galaxy lacked in timing, however, it made up for with technological prowess. The GX-120 was a digital/analog hybrid. It was a digitally switched system that was controlled with a microprocessor and used analog telephones. The new system utilized hardware similar to the SPK's and even had many of the same features but was technically solid where the SPK had been weak. The GX-120 software had been designed by experts who wrote almost flawless code.

"The GX delivered everything that we really wanted to provide in the SPK. We cleaned up the software and invested heavily, and the GX worked. The GX was a stronghold product, and it was very successful, and that got us on the track of being successful," recalled Craig Rauchle, who had been promoted to vice president of the Western Region.[3]

The GX-120 was a major step forward. The system designers, trained in the discipline of software development, had written modular code for the microprocessor. The benefits were twofold. First, Inter-Tel engineers could easily modify the code, identify problems, add features, or otherwise manipulate it. Second, customers could expand or upgrade their systems with software updates, thus eliminating the need to purchase an entirely new system if the company should outgrow its current one.

Like previous Inter-Tel systems, the GX-120 offered features typically reserved for PBX systems, including automatic call distribution, six-digit least-cost routing, call forwarding, hands-free answering, built-in call costing and amplified conferencing. In addition, the GX-120 engineers pioneered a new hardware technology in key-system telephones — the liquid crystal display unit.

"The GX-120 had a liquid crystal display where you could put messages on it," explained Pheanis, who wrote some of the code himself. "So if you were going to leave your phone, you could put it in 'do not disturb' and there were canned messages. Like you could say, 'gone home,' or 'with client,' or 'in meeting' or 'at lunch.'"[4]

Before the GX-120 was released, Pheanis remembered calling Mihaylo into the lab to show him the product. Still in development, the message screen scrolled "gone home with your wife."[5] This practical joke would be remembered only as an amusing sidebar. The GX-120 was remarkably free from bugs. There was a total of 11 errors after in-house testing — an astonishingly low error rate given the bulk of code written to support the system.[6] The new system was so dependable that it led Ray McCloud, who had weathered the SPK crisis on the front line as an installer, to remark, "Life got a lot easier."[7]

"The GX-120 was phenomenally solid right out of the box. It started Inter-Tel's resurrection from ashes," said Jim Chumney, who was hired in 1985 as manager of advanced technologies. "It took a while before people believed that Inter-Tel had turned it around as far as the quality of the design, but it was an extraordinary product."[8]

While the GX-120 addressed the high end of the mid-size market with 32 lines and up to 120 telephones, its counterpart, the Inter-Tel GLX, targeted the smaller user. The GLX expanded to six lines and 12 telephones and offered the small user features usually found on larger systems or expensive add-on equipment. Features included an integrated speakerphone, five-party conferencing, off-premise transfer and a data port.

The Galaxy would be the most successful product family in the company's 16-year history and provide a solid foundation for future products. The success, however, would come too late to prevent an $830,000 loss in

1985.[9] Although it was the third consecutive annual loss, it represented a 65 percent improvement over 1984's $2.4 million loss. Perhaps more importantly, Inter-Tel had regained its reputation as a pioneer and technological innovator.

Maurice Esperseth, who was promoted to executive vice president of research and development in 1986, recalled, "I had the strangest thing happen to me in that I actually had calls from people that wanted to come to work for Inter-Tel because of our reputation and our ASU connection. So many people were working here. They liked the environment. They liked the work they were doing, and I never had that happen to me in my entire life where somebody called me up looking for work, in a job, in an area as scarce as writing software."[10]

Back in the Black

Legend has it that if you walk into a room of Inter-Tel managers and ask them to name Steve Mihaylo's three most cherished buzzwords, they would respond, "staffing, inventory and receivables." The lessons he learned in the early years have become gospel throughout the company. Mihaylo requires his managers to pay close attention to the bottom line. In fact, branch managers are measured by how fast they turn their inventory and collect the receivables. Industry-wide, companies usually turn inventory about 2.5 times. Inter-Tel turns its entire inventory six times every year. For receivables, direct sales operations average about 25 days receivables, while dealers typically average about 60 days. Staffing is held as lean as possible. "That's the trick in business," Mihaylo said. "Grow your sales faster than you grow your head count and expenses."[11]

By the middle of the 1980s, longtime rival TIE/ Communications, which had a larger distribution network, was beginning to fail. TIE/Communications had ballooned to more than $500 million in sales but was poorly managed. It was oversaturated in many of its major markets, forcing TIE dealers to compete against each other.

Inter-Tel was one of the few companies to flourish in the immediate post-AT&T industry. Other companies had expanded to meet the challenge, trying to sell their way out of tough times, and were suffering for it. Steve Mihaylo, on the other hand, cut Inter-Tel back after the SPK crisis, and that decision probably saved the company. By 1986, with a successful new product and confidence once again rippling through the company, Mihaylo was ready to increase the employee level to around 300, including a 40 percent jump in the sales force.[12]

Premier

Inter-Tel's growth was fueled through this period in part because of an OEM agreement with Premier Telecom Products, Inc., a division of North Supply Company, which was a division of Sprint. Mihaylo approached the company in 1986 with the GX-120 and offered Premier exclusive rights to distribute a Galaxy derivative under the name Premier ESP.[13] This repackaging represented the second incarnation of the Galaxy line. To develop the ESP, Inter-Tel used the same software but designed mostly new hardware.

"They just went bananas over the product," recalled Mihaylo. "They loved it. I'm not sure if it was a case of us selling it to them or them talking us into selling it to them, or a combination of the two."[14]

The OEM agreement with Premier was a huge victory for the small company and the largest account ever landed. It began generating income in 1986 and 1987, sometimes accounting for as much as 20 percent of Inter-Tel's revenue.[15] In 1986, Inter-Tel was able to report net income of $400,000. It was the company's first profitable year since 1982.

"The strength that evolved into the GX built our reputation back as a company. GX got us the credibility in terms of the dealers and the end-user customers, and then the ESP really brought us back into the spotlight," recalled Rauchle.[16]

Industry-wide Dogfight

The industry was still shaking itself out after AT&T's divestiture, and competition had become more and more intense. Rampant price-cutting took its toll as competitors fought to see who could hold out the longest. In 1986, the *Arizona Business Gazette* commented on the state of telecommunications companies, describing "warehouses full of products, huge bites in profits, pricing games that went for the throat and an industry-wide dogfight that is still going on, long after many of the once-optimistic players have gone belly-up."[17]

Mihaylo remained among the optimistic. He projected 1987's profits would be four times greater than 1986's. To achieve this, he planned to accelerate the acquisition and partnering program, and even entered international markets in Japan and signed a distribution agreement with Thorn Ericsson, Ltd. in England.

Closer to home, in 1987 Inter-Tel acquired Interconnect Communications Corporation, a Houston-based interconnect company, for 429,989 shares of common stock and $750,069 in cash. Rated by *Telephony* magazine as being among the top 25 interconnect companies in the nation, Interconnect Communications Corporation boasted approximately $4.5 million in sales and offices in Dallas, San Antonio and Houston.[18] "Inter-Tel was represented by Steve Mihaylo and Ralph Marsh," recalled John Gardner, the attorney who represented ICC in the merger. "I had nothing but good impressions of the company."[19]

Gardner's impressions were so good, in fact, that he became the general counsel for Inter-Tel on a part-time basis in 1987. Ten years later, he relocated from Texas to Phoenix to become the full-time general counsel. "I thought Steve Mihaylo was an extremely fine person," Gardner said. "If Steve said something, his word was better than any contract."[20]

The ICC acquisition also brought in knowledge-able executives like Interconnect Communications Corporation's founder and president, Duane Floyd, who was appointed Inter-Tel's senior vice president of direct sales. With 19 years of experience, Floyd went on to head Inter-Tel Communications, the subsidiary formed in the merger.

Inter-Tel would meet Mihaylo's goal of quadrupling net income in one year. Revenues in 1987 rose to $50.1 million with a net income of $2.2 million — a single-year income growth rate of 550 percent.[21] By the end of 1988, Inter-Tel reported revenue of $63.2 million, a 26 percent growth, despite a dip in income to $1.8 million.[22]

Many of the company's competitors, including TIE/ Communications, Executone Information Systems, Inc. (which was acquired by Vodavi in 1987, then merged with ISOTEC in a simultaneous transaction) and NEC Corporation, continued to report losses. According to the Market Research Intelligence Corporation, total revenues of the customer premises equipment market were declining steadily — from $6.1 billion in 1983 to $5.6 billion in 1987. In addition, revenues were expected to hit a low of $5.4 billion the next year.[23]

The 20th Anniversary

Inter-Tel celebrated its 20th anniversary in 1989. It was a good year for the company. Inter-Tel products were well-represented by the Galaxy and the ESP. The distribution network included subsidiaries in Japan and the United Kingdom, 16 direct sales offices in eight states, and a worldwide installed base of more than 100,000 phone systems. Mihaylo, who held about 65 percent of the 8.6 million outstanding shares of Inter-Tel, held the titles of chairman, president and chief executive officer.

As his company had grown, Steve Mihaylo as a manager grew with it. He had started the company by developing his own products, selling the systems and installing them himself. The health of the company rose and fell on his personal tenacity and effort, and he controlled every aspect of Inter-Tel. Over two decades, however, he learned to surrender a certain degree of control to others and manage through consensus building.

As the company rebuilt its reputation, the atmosphere at Inter-Tel relaxed into the style in which Mihaylo had always wanted his company to operate. Describing himself as the "coach," he had never envisioned a workplace that was run by fear — unless it was fear of the marketplace — and the company began to have fun again. At one sales meeting, Mihaylo, Parise, Rauchle and the other top managers staged a mock "deer hunt" for their dealers and distributors, except the hunters emerged from the woods trailing competitor's phones as trophies. At a Halloween party, Mihaylo showed up dressed in drag and managed to make it through the whole party without being recognized.

At work, Mihaylo maintained his open-door policy and still answered his own phone. Jeff Ford, an Inter-Tel engineer recruited by Dave Pheanis, remembered an incident from his early days at the company. He was involved in Junior Achievement and was supposed to give a presentation on business practices. Although he was a design engineer and "in awe of the CEO and original founder," he was able to walk into Mihaylo's office and ask him, "'What does a CEO do?'"

Mihaylo fostered a sense of camaraderie throughout his company and remained confident despite the intense competition choking the industry. In the Phoenix area alone, there were 150 companies selling business telephone systems.[24] In a 1989 interview, Mihaylo remarked, "Except for Inter-Tel, I don't know of a single company making money in our industry now."[25]

For its part, AT&T was doing everything possible to beat down the competition. In a complaint filed with the U.S. Commerce Department, AT&T charged foreign manufacturers with "dumping" products in the American market below manufacturing cost. The decision resulted in an import duty penalty of 13.4 percent on a number of products produced by Inter-Tel's Korean subcontractors.[26] This price increase in manufacturing was partially responsible for 1988-89's decrease in profits even as revenues continued to rise. Almost immediately, Mihaylo shifted to manufacturers in the Philippines and the United States.[27] Profit margins on Inter-Tel's products were already too slim, and the company could not support the import penalty without taking significant losses.

That anniversary year, Maury Esperseth, senior vice president of research and development, decided to retire, although he remained on the board of directors. Commenting on his contribution to the company, Mihaylo said, "He reorganized our engineering department and really turned it into a first-class operation. We didn't become a truly world-class software organization until Maury came along."[28]

Inter-Tel also prepared to release the Premier ESP DX. Like the large-scale GX 400, the ESP DX targeted PBX users with 832 ports. It proved to be a successful product, helping to account for record 1989 fourth quarter sales of $18.6 million.[29] To many people, the period between 1986 and 1989 is when Inter-Tel signaled that it had the technology, the management and the ambition to become a national player in the telecommunica-

The Premier ESP DX and its related family of products helped Inter-Tel maintain profitability as rapidly advancing technology threatened to pass the Galaxy. The market was ready for an all-digital phone system.

tions industry. Although Mihaylo resisted the idea that his company "had arrived," it was clear that Inter-Tel had survived the treacherous growth curve that consumed so many companies of comparable size.

The Digital Revolution

Beginning with Alexander Graham Bell's telephone, the telecommunications industry had been driven by technological innovation. A company like Inter-Tel could never afford to rest on its laurels. In fact, by the last half of the 1980s, the Galaxy and ESP products, even the new ones, had already been surpassed by rapidly advancing technology. "There were all-digital products showing up in 1986 and 1987," remembered Tom Parise.[30] Like all high-tech companies, Inter-Tel

would once again have to innovate to remain viable. Said Jim Chumney:

"What Inter-Tel really needed at the time was a replacement for the GX-120. It needed something that was a fully digital system. The Galaxy was an analog product on the inside. It actually used analog switches to do some switching of the telecom signals. The market was screaming for a digital look-alike to the ESP. When we finally got the ESP DX to market in 1989, it was fairly successful, but it was not nearly as successful as it would have been had we hit the right market segment."[31]

In designing the Galaxy and ESP products, Inter-Tel used analog switching to keep manufacturing costs down. Northern Telecom, however, was taking the market by storm with its digitally switched key-system, Norstar. Other consumer digital products, like compact disc players and clocks, had raised consumer awareness, and the market was beginning to demand digital products.

By the time the ESP DX was on the market, however, Inter-Tel's entire product line was lagging behind the technology curve; the company had not delivered hot new technologies like digital telephones, digital to the desktop, large LCD displays, and use of digital signal processing technology. Also, Inter-Tel had used assembly language to program the Galaxy. By the late 1980s, far more flexible programming languages were coming into favor. Mihaylo and Parise, who had risen to senior management (by 1997, Parise had held 17 different titles in only 17 years), once again sat down to design the next-generation Inter-Tel phone system. According to Parise, Inter-Tel could have introduced a "me too" all-digital product in 1990 or 1991 but instead wanted to design a system that would serve as a new foundation for the company.

> "In the late 1980s, we chartered our best and our brightest engineers with figuring out a whole new system for us, and there were several caveats we wanted in this new system. First of all, we wanted to be extremely open, meaning we could run it on different hardware platforms. We wanted scaleability of software, and we wanted software that was modular. We wanted object-oriented software so we could easily change features. We called it 'features on demand.'"[32]

There was risk involved, but it was of a different kind than Inter-Tel faced when it introduced the first microprocessor-controlled keyset. In those days, it was risky to use a microprocessor at all. By the late 1980s, however, the computer industry was poised to explode, driven by desktop computing, networking, cost-effective power and speed, and user-friendly interfaces.

Industry watchdogs and technologists were already forecasting the day when voice, video and data would all be transmitted over the same lines. And it wouldn't be a phone at the receiving end. It would be a computer. "We firmly believed the computers were going to win the communication game," Parise said. "And we knew it was only a matter of time before the data guys and the PCs and software would be handling the voice side."[33] If Inter-Tel hoped to remain viable in this future marketplace, it needed to design a phone system that could adapt to the unknown. The greatest risk was not competing effectively in the new digital world.

"I remember vividly a time in 1988," Parise said. "Steve and I sat there, and I said, 'Steve, we're going to make the jump.' Steve bet the ranch."[34]

Inter-Tel began a quality process in the late 1980s called Quality First...
Committed to Excellence.

CHAPTER ☎ TWELVE

THE DIGITAL DAWN

"The AXXESS product was not an easy victory. In fact, it missed its scheduled milestones more than once. It became a glorious success, but at the time, we were maybe trying to juggle too many variables at once. We were rewriting the software from scratch. We were redesigning the hardware from scratch. We were adding new technology like digital signal processors. All those things kind of rolled into one. It was a significant challenge to get it to market on schedule."

— Jim Chumney[1]

INTER-TEL ENGINEERS BEGAN DESIGNING AN all-digital phone system in 1988. It would be five years before the company was able to unveil the results of that effort. During those five years, Inter-Tel treaded water on GX and ESP sales, the Galaxy family of products and the OEM agreement with Premier. Revenue rose slightly, but the period of explosive growth had ended, and Inter-Tel wasn't fated to break the $100 million mark in revenue until 1994. The company, it seemed, was in a holding pattern.

Inter-Tel was taking a great risk with a new phone system. The project represented a total overhaul of the product line to keep it current but required a dangerous amount of time in the fast-moving industry and provoked an internal debate. The sales and marketing department pressed for a digital counterpart to the ESP, while the engineering department argued that a digitized ESP would result in a product that was "digital" in name only.

Although there was some attrition in the sales staff, the Inter-Tel team held surprisingly firm throughout this period, especially considering the failure rate among Inter-Tel's contemporaries. By the early 1990s, Inter-Tel was one of the last independent interconnect companies remaining and was in the best position financially and spiritually. Most of the dealers also stayed with the company, and Inter-Tel rewarded them with support services, financial help and other incentives. It is a testament to Inter-Tel's marketing that sales rose, even slightly, as its product line was growing "long in the tooth," as described by Tom Parise.

Nevertheless, the company was under increasing pressure to introduce a "me-too" digital product. But Steve Mihaylo, who personally stood the most to lose by waiting for a new product, didn't agree. He threw his support behind his team of software engineers in developing a completely new product. He reasoned that a digitalized ESP could potentially set the company back because there wouldn't be any foundation for growth.

Supporting a new all-digital product, it turned out, was different from knowing how long it would take to develop one. The company had almost 60 engineers, almost all of whom became involved in the development project at one point or another. With such an ambitious undertaking, projections began at two years and went up from there.

The Purple Heart Acquisition

As the product development team ramped up to produce Inter-Tel's new bread-and-butter phone system, the country limped through a recession. American industry, after two decades of growth and consolidation, began to suffer at the hands of competitive, technologically advanced foreign firms. Desperate to cut costs, U.S. corporations instituted a wide range of efficient manufacturing practices and looked at their huge staffs with a critical eye. It wasn't long before "downsizing" swept into the workplace as corporate America slimmed down to survive in a global economy.

Inter-Tel, however, was in an enviable position. The company kicked off the decade by completing two mergers and founding a subsidiary. In California, Inter-Tel bought Creative TeleSystems. Based in Riverside, Creative TeleSystems was an 18-year-old company with annual sales exceeding $1 million.

In Texas, Inter-Tel acquired a former dealer called Telecommunications Specialists, Inc. (TSI) from Bell Atlantic. The acquisition of TSI, which was renamed Inter-Tel Communications, not only made Inter-Tel a dominant supplier in Texas, but coupled with previous acquisitions made Texas the largest market, with about 30 percent of sales.[2] The acquisition also allowed Inter-Tel to expand into a profitable sideline through the approximately $20 million that TSI had in outstanding lease agreements. Inter-Tel created the Totalease program to enable its customers to lease all their equipment and services under one contract.[3] The lease program was run by TSI vice president Ross McAlpine, who also took responsibility for it at Inter-Tel.

Chuck Oakley also worked for TSI when Inter-Tel bought the company and remembered his first meeting with Mihaylo.

"We had a meeting about inventory or something, and it was the first time we had a one-on-one in his

office. I was awed by looking around at all these pictures of him with notables like Henry Kissinger and Mother Theresa and George Bush. I asked him who was the most impressive individual he'd ever met. He said he thought it was going to be Gandhi for a long time — until he met Mother Theresa."[4]

Inter-Tel offered Oakley a job in the operations side of the business. He accepted, although from his perspective, it seemed that Inter-Tel was a smaller company. "It was a little bit unique from the standpoint that Houston was TSI's corporate headquarters, and it was strange being purchased by Inter-Tel because Inter-Tel's Houston office was small," Oakley said. "We had been selling their products through Premier North Supply."[5]

From the first meeting until the contract was signed, the TSI acquisition took almost a full year and was fraught with challenge. On the first meeting, McAlpine recalled that temperatures in Phoenix soared to 120 degrees, stranding the TSI group in Phoenix because the city had to close its airport. Unbelievably, there wasn't enough lift to allow planes to take off in the thin, hot air. At one point, almost everybody in Inter-Tel was ready to walk away from the deal because of the incredible level of detail that Howard Zuckerman, Bell Atlantic/TSI's point man, was demanding. Craig Rauchle and Ralph Marsh, however, were steadfast in their support for the acquisition. Remembered Oakley:

"The merger was long and drawn out. At the closing dinner afterwards, Steve Mihaylo actually bought real purple hearts, silver stars and even a Congressional Medal of Honor and had them mounted

*and gave them to the people that were involved in
the merger."[6]*

Later that year, Inter-Tel branched out to another
area of telecommunications when the company established the NetSolutions subsidiary to provide long-distance service. The idea that Inter-Tel would buy time
from a long-distance provider like Sprint, MCI or AT&T
originated with Senior Vice President Steve Nichols. It
made Inter-Tel one of the few companies besides AT&T
that offered both telecommunications equipment and
long-distance service.[7] With an estimated hardware
base of 150,000 businesses and about 3 million telephones installed, the long-distance business offered a
substantial market opportunity because it allowed
customers to consolidate their communications needs
with Inter-Tel.[8]

Inter-Tel in 1991 could boast 18 direct sales offices
and around 600 employees. Although the company was
growing, Mihaylo continued to remain accessible to his
employees. He took calls directly from customers and
kept his open-door policy that extended from upper
management to software engineers and beyond. Very
much a hands-on manager, he was reluctant to let his
growing company push him out of the day-to-day operations and consign him to a padded leather chair behind
a mahogany desk.

The company was growing, however, and as a way to
handle the growth, Mihaylo adopted the Philip Crosby
Associates continuous quality process. As opposed to a
"quality program," with a definite ending and starting point,
the quality process at Inter-Tel was built into the company's most fundamental operations. At the same time,
the company slogan was changed to "Quality First ...
Committed to Excellence."

"We're constantly looking for ways to improve in every area," Mihaylo said.

"It's very important everywhere. For example, in accounts receivable. You say, well, what can we do there that's quality? You do it right the first time, which means you always want to make sure that the money for work done is collected as early in the process as possible. Then it never becomes a bad debt. You always correct a problem at the beginning of a process, not at the end. Quality processes are something you bake into your culture."[9]

Land Bust

While 1991 signaled a year of expansion, it also marked a record loss of $4.2 million caused by a $5 million write-down of the company's real-estate holdings.[10] "If it wasn't for our real estate ventures, we would have had nearly $1 million in profits," Mihaylo explained to the *Tempe Daily News*.[11]

In the late 1980s and early 1990s, Arizona property values were driven down by a rash of failed land development. "The problem first surfaced in the office building, apartment and retail mall sectors, where tax-shelter-driven investment unleashed a torrent of new construction activity," explained one *Barron's* journalist. "Office vacancy rates, for example, soared past 20 percent in the Phoenix area by 1986 and remained there because the 1986 Tax Reform Act took away nearly all the tax benefits from such categories of real estate. The absorption rate of new space simply never materialized at expected levels."[12] Predictably, the savings and loan industry reacted to the crashing real estate market with a backlash of foreclosures. Eventually, most of the S&Ls failed, and the

Resolution Trust Corporation (RTC) accelerated the fore-
closure process.

Inter-Tel's $6 million Los Olivios Hotel and office com-
plex, which had been purchased several years before, con-
sistently operated at a loss. Los Olivios turned in only
one profitable quarter in the five years Inter-Tel owned
the property.

"There was a time when all of us had some difficult
times," recalled Bill Bosse. "Obviously you don't build a
company like Mihaylo did without financing, and the
bank at one time was threatening to foreclose on the Los
Olivios property because he had used it as collateral on
a small loan of about $11 million. Here's a city block in
downtown Phoenix, and the bank says it's worthless."[13]

By the end of 1991, Inter-Tel was out of the real
estate business and headed for a record $79.4 million in
revenue for 1992.

Karl Eller Returns to the Board

Inter-Tel was a small company that bred loyalty among
its employees. This culture was driven by Steve Mihaylo,
who was known for his dedication to both his employees
and his friends.

This traditional strength was exemplified in 1992
when Mihaylo asked Karl Eller to return to Inter-Tel's
board of directors. Eller had served on Inter-Tel's
board from 1980 to 1986 and chaired it throughout
the SPK crisis. Between 1986 and 1992, Eller was
consumed by a notorious run as the head of Arizona-
based Circle K Corporation. As CEO, Eller led the con-
venience store chain on a path of rapid growth and
equally rapid descent. Before the end of Eller's tenure,
Circle K racked up more than $1 billion in debt. One
week before the company filed for protection from its

creditors under Chapter 11 of the U.S. Bankruptcy Code, Eller resigned.

The high-profile businessman was immediately the subject of a blizzard of negative media attention. But in the babble of condemning voices, Steve Mihaylo spoke for his friend. "Eller still happens to be the best marketing guy in the valley," he said in *The Phoenix Gazette.*[14] To stockholders who questioned Eller's reappointment to Inter-Tel's board of directors, Mihaylo responded, "I felt, 'Who else would have more finance experience than someone who had built a large business with debt financing?'"[15]

New Distribution Strategy

For six years, Inter-Tel had relied largely on its wholesale agreement with Premier Telecom to move its products to market. The agreement contributed significantly to Inter-Tel's growth, often as much as $25 million in a single year, but by 1991 the drawbacks were beginning to outweigh the benefits. "They wanted a digital product sooner," Mihaylo remarked. "We wanted one that was more state of the art. They weren't willing to wait. So we mutually agreed not to renew the contract."[16]

As Parise put it, cutting out Premier Telecom meant additional profits and greater control of Inter-Tel's market by shifting the sales focus back to the dealer and direct distribution network.

"We were paying somebody a good piece of money to get us to distribution markets," explained Parise. "We had to have more customer control, greater margins, more flexibility. The only way to do that was to have greater control over our own destiny."[17]

The most obvious way to gain control was to establish direct sales offices. That approach, however, was also time-consuming, expensive and fraught with problems. Instead, the company turned back to direct dealers, who weren't owned by Inter-Tel but sold the company's products. By April of 1993, as the contract with Premier expired, the pieces were in place and Inter-Tel re-launched its direct dealer program.[18]

Meanwhile, the company prepared for an offering of 2 million shares of common stock — this time without the expertise of Ralph Marsh, who retired in 1993 to administer Inter-Tel's Employee Stock Ownership Plan. Inter-Tel's challenge was getting the attention of the investment community, according to the new Chief Financial Officer Kurt Kneip.

"The 1993 secondary offering was almost like an initial public offering for Inter-Tel because it had been so long since the IPO; I think the investment community really did not have enough information about our company, and we had no analysts covering us. So there was a challenge of getting the investment community interested at all, but we did have the new digital product offering that was introduced in December of that year."[19]

Investors snapped up the stock at $9.25 a share, and the following month Inter-Tel offered an additional 300,000 shares. The offering raised $20 million.

Digital Signal Processing

By the end of 1993, Inter-Tel was finally ready to release the product that had fueled the successful stock offering. With a five-year development cycle, it took longer than Inter-Tel had hoped to introduce the all-digital AXXESS system, but it was worth the wait. At the time AXXESS was launched, the leading small digital key telephone system on the market was a Toshiba product. Inter-Tel's new product, billed as "the on/off ramp to the emerging digital highway," not only offered the advantages of a truly digital phone system, but laid the foundation for customers to merge their telephones and computers.[20] Supporting 12 to 112 telephones and trunk lines, AXXESS fell in the price range of $6,000 to $50,000.[21]

True to Inter-Tel's track record, AXXESS "jumped the competition" and introduced the use of groundbreaking technology, including the use of object-oriented C++, a new software language that allowed Inter-Tel to support the "feature of the month" simply by writing it into the code. "This was completely new," said engineer Jeff Ford.

> *"The only thing we saved from the old system was the real-time operating system that ran in the CPU. All of the software that controls how features work, user interfaces, that was all brand new. When we rewrote the software, we started with C++, a high level language that was also object-oriented, so it allowed us to add new features more quickly. It was groundbreaking because C++ was being used a little bit in desktop applications like Windows-type applications, but there wasn't really anybody out there using it for embedded real-time systems."[22]*

In addition, Inter-Tel pioneered the use of digital signal processors (DSPs), which were faster than their cousins, the standard microprocessor. Previously, no similarly-sized telecommunications company had used digital signal processors to the extent Inter-Tel was using them.

The ability to handle large amounts of information in a phone system was becoming increasingly important as technology blurred the line between pure data and pure voice. The telephone had come a long way from the rotary dial and electro-mechanical switches and was headed for even more sweeping changes. As one writer hailed, "In the next few years, DSPs will revolutionize telecom in ways most people have not yet even dreamed."[23]

Although Mihaylo had resisted the temptation to churn out a "me-too" digital product that added little functionality, not all telecommunications equipment manufacturers had. The telephone system industry was gripped with "digital hype," with customers demanding digital systems and many companies rushing to market with a "digital" system that was in most ways only comparable to the old analog systems, and in some cases worse.

Computer Telephone Integration

Inter-Tel's AXXESS provided exactly the kind of foundation the company needed for the dawning digital age. Inter-Tel's management team had looked at telecommunications in the late 1980s and had seen that the telephone was headed for a change. In the not-so-distant future, telephone lines would carry a huge variety of data used for computing. This information would pour into standard desk-top computers, which had signaled their supremacy over mainframe computing environments. Traditional voice communication would be only another link in the data chain. Known as "computer telephone integration" (CTI), this movement represented another 66 percent of the total telecommunications market.

The AXXESS system, driven by DSPs, was Inter-Tel's bid to take advantage of that huge opportunity. The system linked data, voice, image and video communications into one network. AXXESS users could link their phone system to their computers and could fax and send data, in addition to standard call and voice processing.

To make AXXESS more accessible, the system had also been designed using open architecture. This allowed Inter-Tel, as well as other software developers, to write custom applications tailored for individual businesses. In the computing and telecommunications environment of the future, success would depend on either establishing the industry standard or conforming to it.

With computer telephone integration and AXXESS, Inter-Tel was challenged to publish the software and make the tools simple enough that MIS people within a company could customize their phone system. The concepts of open architecture and CTI, however, deviated from the telecommunications industry's norm. Telephone experts had to change their mind set and let computers take control. This was a radical shift in perspective for most telephone companies, not just Inter-Tel, and many long-time telephone industry experts were against it.

By the time AXXESS went into development, however, the engineers had more control over what kind of product they would create. For example, during the Galaxy development, the product specifications had been determined by the Product Management Group, which was dominated by sales and marketing experts. These specs were handed down to an engineering department of young, inexperienced programmers. When AXXESS was in development, however, the ASU programmers could rightfully be considered telephony veterans. More and more product functionality was being defined by the engineering group, which accounted for some of the reason the AXXESS software took a quantum leap forward in technology.

Although AXXESS would prove a huge success, it wasn't until the second release of the software that the engineering team's ideas for a computer telephone interface were actually implemented. AXXESS had taken longer than anticipated and, growing impatient, Inter-Tel released the core version of the product without the functionality.

"The AXXESS product was not an easy victory," explained Jim Chumney, then Inter-Tel's senior vice president of engineering. "In fact, it missed its scheduled milestones more than once. It became a glorious success, but at the time, we were maybe trying to juggle too many variables at once. We were rewriting the software from scratch. We were redesigning the hardware from scratch. We were adding new technology like digital signal processors. All those things rolled into one. It was a significant challenge to get it to market on schedule."[24]

As 1993 drew to a close, Inter-Tel was in the strongest financial position in its history.[25] The company had grown to include 18 direct sales offices in the United States, a network of approximately 80 direct dealers and offices in Japan and Europe. Inter-Tel had also expanded its market with NetSolutions and Totalease to include telecommunications services. In its core business, Inter-Tel had carved out a respectable 20 percent of the 25- to 48-line segment of the key telephone systems market,[26] and net sales had climbed to nearly $90 million.

In the 1996 Annual Report, Inter-Tel talks about the "third wave" of telecommunications, characterized by voice, video and data convergence over private intranets or the Internet.

CHAPTER THIRTEEN

A SEA OF CHANGE

"Voice, data and video are all coming together. At some point, we're going to have something that will have the functions of a telephone, a television and a computer all in one device. It's just a matter of time."

— Steve Mihaylo[1]

THE AXXESS SYSTEM HAD AN ELECTRIFYING effect when it hit the market. The tremendous risk shouldered by the Inter-Tel team and by Steve Mihaylo had paid off; AXXESS was a perfect product for its time and was destined to drive Inter-Tel sales up a "hockey stick" graph. Phone system sales had dipped in the late 1980s and early 1990s, but the nation's emergence from the recession and new digital technology unleashed a wave of pent-up demand. With one of the industry's most solid small-scale digital phone systems, Inter-Tel rode the crest and broke $100 million in sales in 1994 — 25 years after Steve Mihaylo sold his first intercom system to Perry Logan at Canyon Ford for $40,000.

"We're just now starting to reach our potential," said Ray McCloud, the manager of the Phoenix branch and

Inter-Tel employee since 1976. "It's actually harder to become a $100 million company when you're a $10 million company than it is to move from a $100 million to $1 billion. We're shooting for those kinds of heights, and I honestly believe this will be a billion dollar company sometime in the early 2000s."[2]

The AXXESS system catered to forward-thinking companies that were interested in merging their various data streams, including fax, voice and video. Computer telephone integration (CTI), once little more than a gleam in an engineer's eye, was hardly new in concept — banks and airlines had already used the technology to make balance and flight information available over the phone — but it had long been restricted to large companies. Inter-Tel's AXXESS changed all that for small and mid-sized companies.

CTI not only allowed a phone system to interact with computers but automated many telephone system functions. One of the most frequently cited examples of CTI was the so-called "screen-pops." With CTI capabilities, a phone system recognized the source of an incoming call, routed it to the correct station, and retrieved that client's file from the company's central computer database, where it popped onto the computer screen. For doctors' offices and companies that received incoming sales calls, the benefits were immediately apparent. The computer could also dial, answer, hold and forward calls using the keyboard or mouse. Dialing was simplified to pointing and clicking on names in on-screen address books.

"A lot of things are coming together," Mihaylo said. "Voice, data and video are all coming together. At some point, we're going to have something that will have the functions of a telephone, a television and a computer all in one device. It's just a matter of time."[3]

As the applications of CTI increased and the price decreased, business owners began to question the idea of keeping their phone systems completely separate from the rest of their network. Some CTI zealots went so far as to question the need for dedicated phone equipment on the desktop at all. Although the dedicated phone handset was far from doomed — traditional phones had 100 years of inertia behind them — CTI technology changed the way people thought about the ubiquitous telephone. "I think a telephone instrument of some sort is always going to exist," said Chief Technology Officer Jeff Ford.

"There's an ease of use with a telephone. There is the privacy issue with handsets. Although there are headsets you can plug into a PC, I doubt anyone would want to have all their conversations over a multimedia PC where it's blasting out into an open room. I think there's always going to be a handset, and it's possible that there might always be a dial pad. There are going to be more and more software applications that will replace telephones, but that transition will be slow."[4]

Even with a "slow transition," the CTI market totaled $1.48 billion in 1995, and the Alliance of Computer-based Telephony Application Suppliers projected it would reach in excess of $7 billion by 1999.[5]

Too Many Bases?

As its new phone system flew off the shelves, Inter-Tel began to refine its focus from phone dealer to overall communications company, offering both equipment and services.

The leasing division was an integral part of this strategy. Under Ross McAlpine, the leasing program was rolled out across the country to all Inter-Tel dealers shortly after the TSI acquisition. A very profitable program, Inter-Tel's leasing program had grown from the original $20 million in outstanding leases to nearly $200 million by 1998 and was continuing to expand. "We use the lease program to differentiate ourselves from the rest of the competition," McAlpine said.

"We don't go in and just try to sell telephone equipment. We're selling telephone service, so included in your lease is the maintenance, insurance and additional training. It's protection against obsolescence. The customer looks at it really much the same way that they looked at the old AT&T years ago. The phone company handles everything for them."[6]

With its NetSolutions division, Inter-Tel also attempted to unite the highly fragmented, and occasionally confusing, telecommunications service market. NetSolutions offered a single source for long-distance service, inbound WATS (1-800 services), outbound WATS (services by which business customers place long distance voice or data calls using either switched or dedicated access), T-1 transmission services and network switching.[7]

Unfortunately, the suggestion by one business journalist that Inter-Tel "might be trying to cover too many bases" carried an element of truth.[8]

NetSolutions had limped out of the starting box and had hobbled along ever since. Inter-Tel's Senior Vice President Steve Nichols struggled to get NetSolutions off the ground, but the unit ran into competitive pressures and lackluster support from Inter-Tel's sales force. The problem, as Craig Rauchle explained it, was that

NetSolutions suffered from a lack of national support across the company's sales force. No longer a spunky start-up, Inter-Tel was confronting the challenges of growth and found it difficult to rally its far-flung troops around a service offering that was foreign to them.

Nichols, however, was unwilling to give up on NetSolutions. "He felt there was still a pony in the barn," Rauchle said, "but he felt it would probably be better to be supported directly out of Phoenix, and that's when the control got turned over to Tom Parise and NetSolutions was moved to Phoenix."[9]

Parise, however, was deeply involved in strengthening the dealer distribution network. The Premier contract was lapsing, and Inter-Tel needed an alternative network in place. As a result, NetSolutions got shuffled to the back burner. Then, in 1994, Mihaylo brought in his younger brother Chuck to focus full-time on the project.

"They weren't making any money with it," recalled Chuck. "And everybody in the company started trying to play with it to see if they could get the thing to work. Nobody really wanted it. Nobody, except Steve, felt it was something that should be part of Inter-Tel because it was an equipment/software manufacturer and this was the other side of the business. So when I came to Inter-Tel, I came here knowing that we either shut this down and confirm what everybody else thinks or make it work."[10]

Chuck approached the problem from several angles. First, he asked Steve to help him focus on the sales force to convince them that Inter-Tel was a communications company, not just a hardware/software provider. He also switched from Sprint as a dedicated long-distance provider to MCI, which was willing to provide the dedicated lines Inter-Tel wanted. John O'Block, who had worked with Chuck for almost eight years, was brought into NetSolutions in 1994 to help. "The NetSolutions charter was to build the business, but make a profit rather than just build bulk," O'Block said.[11] It worked. In 1994, NetSolutions experienced a 16 percent gain and grew to sales of $4.3 million.[12] Within three years, NetSolutions was growing faster than the rest of Inter-Tel with the same profit margin.

Although it represented only a fraction of Inter-Tel's revenue, NetSolutions provided important foreshadowing. "We'd better recognize that we're in the communication industry and not just in the equipment hardware/software business," said Chuck Mihaylo, "because here at Inter-Tel, hardware is going to start disappearing."[13] NetSolutions, a service organization from the beginning, was in a tremendous position to benefit from the combination of Internet-based communications and more traditional avenues of long-distance service.

Passing the Baton

With the exception of a two-year stint in the early 1980s, Steve Mihaylo had spent 25 years as Inter-Tel's sole president, CEO and chairman of the board. It was his company from top to bottom, with his influence setting the tone and direction. By 1994, however, he was ready to take his first steps away from the day-to-day operations and entrust more control to the team of loyal executives that had coalesced around him. In 1994, Mihaylo and Inter-Tel's board appointed Tom Parise Inter-Tel's third president.

"Inter-Tel's executive staff is able to react very quickly and intelligently," remarked John Gardner, Inter-Tel's general counsel since 1986.

"There are just a small handful of executives around Steve, and they move very quickly, very knowledgeably

onto anything that needs to be dealt with. Ten years ago, when we were being compared to Executone or TIE, we left them in the dust, even if we didn't have the sales that they did at the time. We're the only one of that group that's had the profitability and the growth and the emerging technology over the last eight or ten years. The reason for that would be because of Steve, Tom and Craig and all of the executive officers and their ability to move on anything and in any area."[14]

As the newly appointed president, Parise became the logical successor to one day inherit the top position at Inter-Tel. A Coca-Cola regional manager who 15 years earlier had insisted that Inter-Tel hire him, Parise had worked his way from a sales representative to the company president and chief operating officer. "I think in our course of action we've taken calculated risks," Parise said. "We've really minded our Ps and Qs. We've kept our powder dry. That's why we've done well, while our competitors have fallen by the wayside. That's really important."[15]

Mihaylo and Inter-Tel's board also promoted another Inter-Tel loyalist, Craig Rauchle, then president of Inter-Tel's Western United States direct sales subsidiary, to the position of executive vice president. In Rauchle's 18 years with Inter-Tel, he had journeyed from branch manager of Denver's direct sales office to vice president of the Western region and finally to executive vice president. In addition to being well-suited to head the company's acquisition strategy, Rauchle also possessed Mihaylo's frugal nature.

"I think I was also fortunate in being shrewd like Steve in terms of what we were willing to pay for our acquisitions. I negotiated deals that were favorable to Inter-Tel and met our targets," he said.[16] In his new position, Rauchle headed the company's active expansion plan. The number of Inter-Tel's direct sales offices rose from 21 in 1994 to 30 in 1996, and the company entered several new markets.

Inter-Tel broke into the New Mexico market via the acquisition of Southwest Telephone Systems, Inc. — a company serving approximately 2,500 customers with 1993 revenues exceeding $4 million.[17] In Georgia, Inter-Tel expanded into the marketplace with the acquisition of American Telecom Corporation of Georgia, Inc. — a company with $6 million in revenues in 1994.[18]

In Ohio, Inter-Tel purchased long-time dealer Bill Nicewanger and his partner, Ray Lewis', $9 million business, NTL Corporation (ComNet of Ohio), with its two direct sales offices.[19] ComNet's offices established Inter-Tel's third market between New Jersey and St Louis. "From the point of view of culture, there were relatively few changes after Inter-Tel acquired us," said Nicewanger. "We had been a dealer of Inter-Tel's all the way back into the 1970s, and so we felt as if we knew the company and were able to be fairly assured that the culture of the two companies was similar."[20]

By the end of 1996, Inter-Tel had direct sales offices in 25 major markets and a growing network of more than 1,000 dealers. In addition, the company established 20 dealers in Europe, a direct office in the United Kingdom, and a dealer and a direct sales office in Japan, and signed three more dealers in Asia.[21]

Although Inter-Tel had come a long way from its humble start in a small office, it was still a modest company compared to giants like AT&T and Lucent — but for the first time, Inter-Tel technology invited comparison.

"Our biggest challenge is growth," said Chuck Oakley, vice president of operations. "I don't think there's ever going to be a clear, defined channel of distribution between dealers and direct offices. Our direct offices handle about

60 percent of our business. We send a lot of our new products through both channels."[22]

New AXXESS

During this period of rapid geographic expansion and new products, Inter-Tel began to reach beyond its traditional market of small- to mid-size businesses. Although Inter-Tel ranked second behind Northern Telecom in the 24- to 48-line market, and third in the 9- to 24-line market, its offerings were somewhat limited in the largest and most profitable segment — telephone systems above 48 lines.[23]

Hoping to gain share in the more lucrative market for larger systems, Inter-Tel released the AXXESS 3.0 software. A software upgrade for the system, AXXESS 3.0 represented Inter-Tel's first step in eliminating the AXXESS size cap. Previously limited to 112 lines, the AXXESS 3.0 software increased the system's capacity to 256 ports.

While AXXESS 3.0 sought share in the most profitable segment of the market, a new product release called the AXXENT pursued the $1.4 billion market of systems with less than 16 telephones.[24] Basically a low-end version of the AXXESS, the AXXENT brought an affordable digital system with CTI capabilities, voice mail, speakerphones and caller ID to the 4- to 16-line market.

Although both AXXESS and AXXENT gained market share for Inter-Tel at the hardware end of the business, the lion's share of the market was shifting from hardware to software and services. In 1996, industry analysts predicted a meager 6.6 percent growth rate in traditional telephone hardware. Comparatively, CTI hardware and software were anticipated to grow at a 78 percent compounded annual growth rate, from $130 million in 1994 to $1.3 billion in 1998.[25]

The market shift didn't come as a surprise to companies like Inter-Tel, which had begun shifting towards integration software in the mid-1980s. It did, however, bring a new set of challenges. As ASU professor Dr. Dave Pheanis explained, "The change is so rapid that all software-intensive companies struggle to keep up. You can conceive something a lot more quickly than you can implement and build it."[26]

The Telecommunications Act of 1996

Since the introduction of competition in the late 1960s, the telecommunications industry had endured the tumultuous upheavals created by deregulation, the divestiture of AT&T, and the endless waves of competitors. In 1996, yet another change was about to alter the landscape — the Telecommunications Act of 1996.

Although the 1984 divestiture of AT&T changed the way the communications market operated, legislation such as the Communications Act of 1934 still retained its influence on the shape of the industry. Drafted while AT&T still enjoyed its monopoly status, the Communications Act of 1934 was based on the idea that building competing networks was a waste of resources.[27] Its main consideration was not competition but assurance that everybody in the United States had access to quality telephone services.

The Telecommunications Act of 1996, however, sought to infuse the missing elements of competition and deregulation into the changing industry. The first paragraph of the Act summarized the goal of the new law: "To provide for a pro-competitive deregulatory national policy framework designed to accelerate rapid private sector deployment of advanced telecommunications and information technologies and services to all Americans by opening all telecommunications markets to competition."[28]

In its effort to break the industry wide open, the Telecommunications Act of 1996 tore down many of the walls that had been in place for more than 60 years. It mandated that the huge local service providers would have to provide discounts to competitors that wanted to interconnect into their networks, which had the possible effect of allowing long-distance companies into local telephone service. Revising the Communications Act of 1934, the Telecommunications Act of 1996 also allowed the various other segments of the communications industry — wireless companies, cable TV providers and more — to offer telephone service.

While the new law in some ways hailed opportunity, it also increased competition. "It's clear that in the not-so-distant future, the lion's share of the market will go to firms that can offer the widest array of telecom products and services," wrote John Simons for *U.S. News & World Report.* "Rather than create costly systems from scratch, companies will more likely team up to win customers. There are currently some 20 large-scale enterprises in the $175 billion U.S. communications industry. But according to Dan Merriman of Giga Information Group, a technology research firm, a flurry of mergers and acquisitions is about to change that — and rather quickly. 'Within the next three years,' predicts Merriman, 'there will be just three to five large national communications superpowers.'"[29]

Looking to capture early market share, cable companies, long-distance providers and local telcos touched off a spree of mergers and acquisitions as they jumped at the opportunity to become "one-stop" communications providers. The industry's first company to offer local and long-distance service and Internet access was formed when WorldCom, the nation's fourth largest long-distance provider, merged with MFS Communications, a local telco and Internet provider in 14 metropolitan areas.[30]

"The passage of the Bill prompted a wave of change," said *Financial Executive Magazine.* "Every week brings another announcement of a merger or acquisition. Bell Atlantic and Nynex, two of the regional Bell operating companies, have merged. U.S. West is acquiring Continental Cablevision. The three major long-distance providers — AT&T, MCI and Sprint — plan to launch their attacks on the local telephone markets."[31] In late 1997, MCI and WorldCom announced a merger, and Bell Atlantic negotiated another merger with GTE to provide long-distance service and local service. Within another year, AT&T had kicked off an ambitious round of acquisitions.

After the initial spree of activity, however, the sweeping changes that the Act promised became mired in a sea of slow-moving regulatory reform. In September 1996, much of the bill was suspended in the 8th U.S. Circuit Court of Appeals in St. Louis, leaving the states to concoct their own pricing rules for local telephone service. This prompted more legislation as the major companies filed more than 100 cases protesting state-mandated pricing rules over the next two years. The case finally went to the Supreme Court, which was expected to rule in 1999 on who has the authority to deregulate local telephone service. Until then, and maybe even after, the changes envisioned by the bill's authors remain an uncertainty.

Running Flat Out

Well-intentioned as it may have been, a new telecommunications act wasn't needed to stimulate competition. Technology was moving at blinding speed as the entire landscape of communications changed. Products that often took years to develop faced the likely threat of becoming obsolete within a year of hitting the market. No one knew for sure which emerging technology would dominate. The breakneck pace, however, was nothing new for Inter-Tel. "Inter-Tel runs the way it does because of technology and competition," said Mihaylo. "Managers in this business don't need to use fear to motivate. There's enough competitive pressure outside the company. We manage by fear of the marketplace."[32]

As Inter-Tel entered 1997, the company gambled again on a growing segment of the marketplace — the Internet.

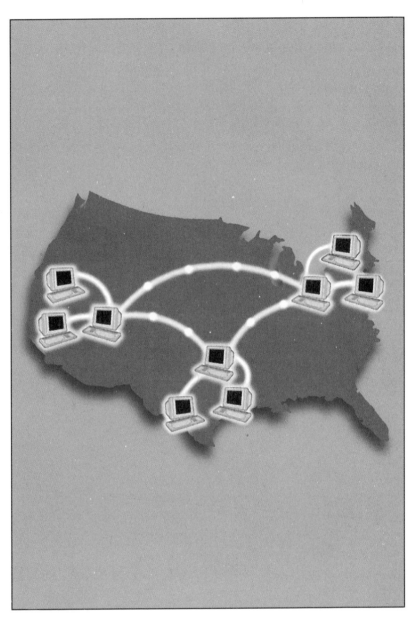

As the Internet gained widespread acceptance and voice-over-the-Internet became a reality, Inter-Tel unveiled its proprietary voice network, called Inter-Tel.net, which used an Internet technology called Vocal'Net to harness the power of a worldwide data network.

CHAPTER FOURTEEN

IP, IP and Away!

"The long-distance companies are against [Internet tele-phony] because it potentially could destroy their markets."

— Steve Mihaylo[1]

IN THE LATE 1990s, COMPANIES LIKE INTER-TEL had to pick and choose which segments of the rapidly merging market to pursue. Wireless communication will someday soon blend with the Internet, which will carry real-time voice and video; and e-mail will be sent and received from cellular phones. And, overshadowing everything, the prospect of Internet telephony loomed large in the imagination of both communications companies and the public.

Going into 1997, Inter-Tel was in a good position to pursue a risky new venture. With more than $200 million in AXXESS-driven sales, Inter-Tel boasted an average growth rate of at least 20 percent, while the employee level hovered slightly below 1,200 with an engineering staff of more than 100. Unlike heads of comparably sized companies, Mihaylo kept staffing at Inter-Tel "so lean that there's little chance of a layoff."[2]

The Internet

Only a few short years after its commercial introduction, the Internet was well on its way to revolutionizing the nature of communication networks. But surprisingly, the theory behind the public data network almost met its end on a dusty shelf in the federal government's Information Processing Techniques Office.[3]

In the late 1960s, a computer scientist named Paul Baran devised a communications network that radically departed from AT&T's traditional centralized design. Using the human brain as a model, Baran theorized that decentralizing a communication network would decrease its vulnerability. Instead of a centralized system where all transmissions were routed through a central point, Baran's network resembled a fishnet or neural network, each point having numerous paths to one another. With more than one route to a destination, a decentralized network could sidestep inoperable points just as the brain can find ways around a damaged region.[4]

While Baran believed a decentralized network could make data communications more reliable and efficient, convincing AT&T (the only company with the resources and know-how to finance such a network) was another story.

"Their attitude was that they knew everything and nobody outside the Bell system knew anything," remarked Baran in the book, *Where the Wizards Stay Up Late.* "And somebody from the outside couldn't possibly understand or appreciate the complexity of the system. So here some idiot comes along and talks about something being very simple, who obviously does not understand how the system works."[5]

As if trying to convince AT&T that its network was inferior wasn't enough to get him booted out of Ma Bell's offices, Baran proposed breaking data messages into small blocks or packets. The dedicated lines of AT&T's circuit-switched network, he reasoned, wasted line capacity (or bandwidth) because they devoted an entire line to each call for the full duration of the call. Regardless of whether that line was transmitting information or silence, the line remained occupied. Breaking messages into small blocks and sending them through a decentralized network, however, allowed message blocks to slip into the inherent pauses in data communications. In addition, a message block had multiple routes to its destination, and if one route was full, it could select another. Baran's model, later termed "packet switching," allowed more information to be sent over the same number of lines.[6]

A good analogy of a circuit-switched network versus Baran's packet-switched network is a freeway. With a circuit-switched network, only one car at a time can occupy a freeway lane. That car cannot change lanes and is the only occupant from the beginning to the end of its journey. Only when the car exits can another car use its lane. On the freeway represented by Baran's model, however, cars travel bumper to bumper, dart into spaces left open in other lanes and seek their destination by the quickest possible route.

While AT&T essentially laughed Baran out of its offices for his packet-switching theory, a 41-year-old physicist at the British National Physical Laboratory (NPL) named Donald Davies was having more luck with the British telecommunications establishment. Unaware of each other's work, Baran and Davies developed strikingly similar theories. Like Baran, Davies devised a model of breaking messages into packets of information to utilize bandwidth. Unlike Baran, however, Davies found funding for an experimental network.

While Davies tinkered on his experiments, Baran's work ended up on a shelf in the Information Processing Techniques Office. Months passed before the idea of a packet-switching network finally fell into the hands of Larry Roberts, a program director for the U.S. Department of Defense's Advance Research Projects Agency (ARPA). Roberts was faced with the challenge of building a communications network that could link research computers of the nation's universities. The idea was to share resources and reduce redundant research. Without the link, many universities applied for grants on research another university had already done. The mission at ARPA was to unite the universities into a team.

Linking computers hundreds of miles away, however, had never been done, and Roberts had more on his hands than the miles separating the universities. He also had to contend with the fact that universities used different computers and they did not all necessarily speak the same language.

Roberts gathered information on computers and networking from every corner of the scientific community. He hired Baran as a consultant and frequently referred to Davies' published manuscripts. Roberts and a team of engineers spent close to a year researching and assembling the ARPA network or ARPAnet. On November 21, 1968, a half dozen scientists gathered in UCLA's Boelter Hall and watched as the first long-distance computer-to-computer communication occurred. None of them could realize the impact their success would have on the future of communications.[7]

The original ARPAnet linked four computers including the University of Utah, Stanford Research Institute, University of California at Santa Barbara and UCLA. By 1971 there were nearly two dozen sites, including machines at MIT and Harvard. Three years later there were 62 and by 1981, more than 200.[8]

The success of the ARPAnet inspired additional networks, including efforts by several foreign governments and a growing number of corporations. As separate networks began to grow, two computer networking specialists named Bob Kahn and Vint Cerf began to consider the possibility of connecting the multiple networks together. The main obstacle was that differing networks often used different networking protocols. For them to interact, they needed a common language.

Hoping to overcome the language barrier, Kahn and Cerf developed TCP/IP, or Transmission Control Protocol/ Internet Protocol. TCP/IP handled packets so they could travel across network lines by inserting a header, or address, on each data packet to indicate its origination and destination. Computers that linked two or more networks had only to read the header, not the message itself. It worked much like the postal system, with letters traveling from one hub to another according to the information contained on the outside envelope. Only when the letter reached its destination was it opened and read. As long as the envelope was addressed in the proper language, it did not matter if the letter itself was in English or Japanese. TCP/IP effectively shifted the responsibility of translating the messages from the gateway computers to the end computers.[9]

With the invention of TCP/IP, a network of networks was now possible, and Internet usage began to climb. The real boost in user numbers, however, came after the Mosaic graphical browser was introduced in 1993. Developed by a group of graduate students at the University of Illinois, Mosaic extended the boundaries of the World Wide Web beyond the academic and scientific communities to the public.[10] Suddenly the Internet became accessible to just about anyone with a person-al computer.[11]

In 1996, 19 million worldwide used the Internet.[12] By the end of 1998, the number of connected people had soared to more than 67 million people, and some esti-mates project one billion people online by 2000.[13] The Internet offered a vast opportunity to transform the world of communication. E-mail became a popular application — contributing to the U.S. Postal Service's $1.8 billion loss between 1990 and 1993[14] — and applications for sending voice over the Internet were not far behind.

Internet Telephony

Lured by free access to the public network, an Israeli company named Vocaltec began experimenting with send-ing voice communications over the Internet. If information could be sent over the network, why not voice? Science had devised a way to digitize voice, so why not use the Internet to circumvent high long-distance charges?

When it came to Internet telephony, however, there was one problem. The very nature of packet-switching, or breaking messages into bits and sending them on mul-tiple paths to a destination where they were reassem-bled, didn't cater well to voice transmissions. The data packets that comprised a message did not necessarily arrive at the same time. Nor did they arrive in order. The end of a message might arrive a second before the mes-sage's start. This created a delay as all of the pieces of a message waited patiently to be united into a coherent communication. Although the lag times created did not impact data transmissions, they were a serious obstacle to sending voice transmissions.

Despite the obstacles, Vocaltec introduced the first application for Internet telephony, the Internet Telephone, in 1995. Although the Internet Telephone's transmission was broken and gravel-voiced, free long-distance calls offered enough incentive to overlook the new technology's shortcomings, and Internet telephony took root.

Traditional long-distance carriers like AT&T remained surprisingly cool towards the new technology. Firmly rooted in circuit-switching technology, AT&T held its ground that packet-switching was and always would be inferior and that the Internet was little more than a toy for hacks. AT&T already had turned its back on the Internet in 1971 when it declined ARPA's offer to own and operate the network.[15] As far as AT&T was concerned, Internet telephony had a long way to go before it could present a threat.

"We're looking at it but aren't overly concerned. It's not in our league," reported one AT&T spokesperson in 1995.[16]

Skeptics were quick to point out the technology's limitations. First, people couldn't place a call unless the intended subject was waiting on-line. Second, the voice quality suffered from static, pops and crackles. Third, the delay represented between 200 and 500 milliseconds for domestic calls and between 500 milliseconds and a whopping 1.5 seconds for international calls. Finally, the lack of industry standards made communicating between Internet telephony applications impossible.[17]

Small, innovative companies and universities addressed these problems incrementally. By 1997, voice transmissions had improved to near-cellular quality and lag times had decreased. In addition, the industry defined a standard called H.323 that, once implemented, allowed different applications to talk to one another.

Inter-Tel and the Net

Inter-Tel watched the development of Internet telephony closely. The company had been on the public network since 1985 when it connected to a machine at ASU, and saw the potential inherent in a vehicle for free mass communication. As more people signed on and the quality of Internet telephony steadily improved, Inter-Tel decided it was time to throw its hat into the ring.

In October 1997, Inter-Tel released its Internet telephony product, Vocal'Net.[18] True to the inertia of the past decade, Vocal'Net had a very high software content. "But there are pretty hefty digital signal processing boards involved," said Mark Hamblin, a software engineer who worked on the project in 1998. "The reason we need hardware is because it's a server. It's not like your Internet telephone like Net Media or Cool Talk or whatever you get on a PC. Vocal'Net can handle 24 simultaneous calls and, in the future, will be able to handle even more than that."[19]

Vocal'Net was a powerful, large-scale product designed with phone companies in mind. Instead of competing with them, Inter-Tel hoped to find a market with long-distance providers and cable companies. "It's a companion product," said Jeff Ford, who had been elevated to chief technology officer. "We're able to sell equipment to companies that may want to set up a network say in Sweden and put our product in Sweden to route calls there."[20]

Shortly after its release, Vocal'Net was hailed as one of the best Internet telephony products available. In addition to what *Computer Telephony* magazine characterized as "superb" sound,[21] Vocal'Net offered its customers one of the easiest systems on the market to install and use. By the end of the year, Vocal'Net drew some of the industry's top honors including "Product of the Year" from *Computer Telephony* magazine and "Editors Choice" from *CTI* magazine.[22]

The product also attracted the attention of Microsoft Chairman Bill Gates, who visited Inter-Tel's booth at Comdex 1996, the world's largest computer industry trade show. Gates, who chooses only 10 exhibits a year to visit, was reportedly following Inter-Tel's progress carefully because the system used Windows NT.

Internet telephony was becoming a hot industry very quickly. Consultants and analysts predicted Internet telephony could grow to be a $10 billion market by 2000, while more optimistic estimates reached to $53 billion annually by 2002.[23] "The world has opened up because everybody in the world is interested in this," said Mike Sargent, vice president of marketing.

"Six years ago, it was primarily a domestic market. Now with Vocal'Net, it's scalable from very small to extremely large. We're able to meet the needs of Fortune 500 companies, and we're also able to reach the consumer because we're selling to companies who sell this directly to the consumer, whether it's a long-distance service over an IP telephony network or it's something supplied through cable television. We're fishing in the ocean now instead of a pond."[24]

Companies that had once written off the technology began to scramble, and the media helped fuel the frenzy as leading business publications such as *Barron's* announced Internet telephony with a flourish:

"IP telephony's arrival will hurl shock waves across the telecommunications landscape. The technology will provide a bonanza for equipment makers, save billions of dollars for consumers and corporations and spur development of new services and upstart carriers. The pecking order in global telecommunications has already begun to shift, and the Internet has been no small factor."[25]

This shift in telecommunications did, indeed, have profound effects on the U.S. communications market.

The spree of acquisitions and mergers continued as cable and traditional data companies partnered with telephone giants, each trying to establish itself as the largest data carrier. Between 1996 and 1999, more than $50 billion in acquisitions were announced by various elements of the communications industry reaching for dominance in the new market.

As one of only a handful of companies with Internet telephony applications on the market, Inter-Tel had an early head start on its competitors. Michael Shonstrom, an analyst with Neidiger Tucker Bruner, remarked: "There are a number of companies out there attempting to develop products to take advantage of this market. It appears to me that Inter-Tel has sort of snuck up on them and developed a beachhead that is far and away a great advancement over what everyone else is doing."

Investors agreed. In September 1997, stock prices soared 19 percent in one week, reaching a 52-week two-for-one split-adjusted high of $18.88, and an additional 3 million shares of common stock released on the market in November were gobbled up at $21 per share.[26]

Sales also skyrocketed. In 1997, the company achieved the highest revenues and profits in its history. Net income soared to $14.7 million, an increase of 62 percent over 1996, and net sales grew to $223.6 million.

Inter-Tel.net

While AXXESS remained Inter-Tel's core business, Mihaylo led the company further into the software and services realm. The number of mergers and alliances between cable companies, long-distance providers, Internet service providers and local telcos reflected the industry's shift toward a single-source mentality, and Mihaylo worked to position the company in the new arena.

Inter-Tel's long-distance subsidiary, NetSolutions, had undergone a rocky start but by 1996 was growing at more than twice the rate of Inter-Tel and generating revenues of $12 million, but it was still reselling time from other providers.[27] Mihaylo felt that the company could set up its own Internet long-distance service and entice even more customers.

Inter-Tel soon established a series of Vocal'Net servers through which customers could dial into the Inter-Tel proprietary network.

Dubbed Inter-Tel.net, the network established its first nodes in Phoenix, San Jose, New York City, Chicago, Washington, D.C., and Los Angeles. It was placed under the leadership of Ross McAlpine, president of Inter-Tel Leasing and Inter-Tel Net Solutions. In 1998, the Inter-Tel.net network took its first international steps when NTT International Corporation, a subsidiary of the world's largest telecommunications company, Nippon Telephone and Telegraph, agreed to set up a similar network in Japan.[28] Throughout the next year, Inter-Tel rapidly signed on international partners with POP (point of presence) hubs that could hook into Inter-Tel's growing IP telephony network, and invested heavily in building the network.

As with any Internet telephony product, there was lag time in the system, and the quality of the voice transmission was roughly equivalent to a cellular phone. But the possible savings were tremendous, and by the middle of 1999, Inter-Tel was able to offer among the highest quality Internet voice transmissions by souping up the system with powerful, dedicated microprocessors.

"The Death of the Internet"

As companies like Inter-Tel began to offer cheaper alternatives to the traditional circuit-switched network, a small percentage of voice traffic shifted to the Internet, and industry observers predicted the inevitable decline of the old telephone network. While many agreed the shift in communications was bound to happen, estimates as to how much and how soon differed. In 1997, *Fortune* predicted that 18.5 percent of all domestic phone traffic would be carried over data networks by 2002.[29] Vint Cerf, one of the inventors of TCP/IP, however, painted a more optimistic picture.

"While voice traffic has been growing at about 7 percent, data traffic has been growing at 300 percent," remarked Cerf. "That means the Internet will pass by the phone network (in traffic volume) sometime around 2000 or 2001. Pretty quickly thereafter, voice will really just be ancillary traffic."[30]

Companies like Inter-Tel gambled on the Internet's success, yet others questioned whether the network could handle the load. Articles like "Death of the Internet," which appeared in *Popular Mechanics*, foretold of the overburdened and overworked Internet's doom.

> *"Considering the demands that have been placed on the Internet — the number of users is growing at an annual rate of about 200 percent — it's remarkable that it has managed to keep up at all. In addition, the range of services that the Internet is providing was never envisioned by the people who developed what has grown into today's Net."[31]*

With this much speculation and potential surrounding Internet telephony, it was only a matter of time until traditional phone companies felt threatened. "The long-distance companies are against it because it potentially could destroy their markets," said Steve Mihaylo.[32]

Local telcos began lobbying the FCC for regulations, arguing that Internet users tied up the lines for hours at a time and that Internet service providers should be required to pay a fee for using those lines just as long-distance carriers did.[33] As it stood, local telcos were out of the loop.

Although still unregulated in 1999, Internet telephony manufacturers and service providers feared the specter of change hovering over them. The government, for the time being, also appeared unwilling to regulate the Internet. At a 1996 INET conference in Montreal, FCC Chief of Staff Blair Levin said:

> *"On the Internet, voice traffic is just a particular kind of data, and imposing traditional regulatory divisions on that data is both counterproductive and futile. ... More importantly, we shouldn't be looking for ways to subject new technologies to old rules. Instead, we should be trying to fix the old rules so that if those new technologies really are better, they will flourish in the marketplace. ... Internet telephony may well become, in time, a competitive alternative to traditional circuit-switched voice telephony."*[34]

With a blend of products that included hardware, software, networking applications and IP telephony service, Inter-Tel had capitalized on the "third wave" in telecommunications technology and matured into a one-stop communications provider.

CHAPTER FIFTEEN

THE THIRD WAVE

"Things are changing so rapidly that somebody could leapfrog us. That's how quickly change occurs, but on the other hand it's a huge marketplace that could be hundreds of billions of dollars worldwide, maybe even approaching a trillion dollars. There's going to be a lot of room for a company like ours."

— Steve Mihaylo[1]

H EADING INTO ITS 30TH YEAR IN BUSINESS, Inter-Tel looked forward to the coming years with anticipation. Although competitive pressures in the market weren't expected to ease, Inter-Tel had finally reached a size from which it could contemplate serious acquisitions. And CEO Steve Mihaylo and his management team already had a few targets in mind. This strategy, coupled with the development of new business opportunities and the further development of the AXXESS platform, promised rapid and rational growth. To accommodate some of the expected new business, Inter-Tel built an office complex in Reno, Nevada.

The year 1998 began with an early surprise, however, when Tom Parise, the popular president of Inter-Tel, resigned for personal reasons, although he continued to maintain a close relationship with Steve Mihaylo and his company. For Inter-Tel, the loyalties of the previous two decades paid off handsomely, and Mihaylo was able to draw new leadership from a cadre of experienced and dedicated executives. Jeff Ford was named president of Inter-Tel Integrated Systems, which meant he was still in charge of the engineering operation. Inter-Tel.NET and the leasing division were consolidated under Ross McAlpine, who held the titles of president of Inter-Tel Leasing, Inter-Tel NetSolutions and Inter-Tel.NET. Craig Rauchle remained in charge of Inter-Tel's direct sales operation. Finally, Mihaylo asked Norman Stout, an Inter-Tel board member since 1994, to accept the position of president of Inter-Tel's Software and Services operations.

Before joining Inter-Tel's board, Stout had been running the $500 million U.S. operations of an Irish company that sold concrete block and pavers. He met Mihaylo through the Young Presidents' Organization, and the two found they shared a passion. "Steve and I started talking about balance sheet issues, controlling inventories and receivables," Stout said. "He has a real passion for that, as do I, and also about controlling costs."[2] When Stout joined the company in 1998, he assumed responsibility for the general operation of Inter-Tel in a "kind of three-way presidency" with Mihaylo and Rauchle.

"When I joined, Inter-Tel was just starting to grow a lot, outgrowing office space, outgrowing its accounting system," Stout said. "And I'd already grown a company like that. So this gave me an opportunity to join an organization that was exciting and fast growing on the one hand, and on the other hand needed a professional manager who had done this before."[3]

This team of executives was in a position to help Inter-Tel grow into the shape that had been planned for it so many years before. As the company solidified its position as a one-stop communications provider, it was clear that Inter-Tel had matured. Predictions that the company would soon break the $1 billion mark became ever more frequent.

Many observers confidently predicted that Inter-Tel would engineer a major acquisition using some of its growing financial clout. Not that it had many peers left to acquire — Inter-Tel had nearly become the "last man standing." Over the previous three decades, many of the small telephone system interconnect equipment companies that had sprung up on the heels of the Carterfone decision had either been acquired or gone under because of poor management. The remaining ones were often severely weakened.

Instead, Inter-Tel's traditional competitors had been replaced by telecommunications giants like Nortel, Cisco Systems and Lucent. And, at least in Inter-Tel's traditional strength of small to mid-size business phone systems, even the big players found the market treacherous and uncertain. In mid-1999, Lucent announced it was divesting its entire phone system group that served small and mid-size businesses. The newly independent company, called Avaya, with phone system sales of almost $850 million, became the largest player in the market overnight — but the divestiture was seen as a tacit acknowledgement that Lucent wasn't winning in the market.

In another signal that Inter-Tel had arrived, these companies didn't compete solely in the market for business phone systems. They competed for the opportunity to service entire sets of communications needs, for the chance to own the hardware, software and multiple avenues that companies used to communicate.

When competing in a fierce communications market with billion-dollar giants looking to acquire their way into emerging markets, Inter-Tel counted on the strength of its management. Steve Mihaylo, now a seasoned CEO of an expanding company, had learned much from the growing years, and his company remained an exciting, fun place to work. It was often compared to a family by the people who worked there. "We've always had a family atmosphere," Mihaylo said. "We've done it by being very involved with our associates, the people who work for Inter-Tel. But we're not just a big family with no discipline and no hierarchy. We've got a lot of discipline as a company."[4]

In July 1998, Inter-Tel celebrated a technological milestone with the release of the AXXESS 5.0 software — and really signaled it was ready to compete with the big players. This newest software represented years of ambition and offered tremendous flexibility to customers. Through AXXESS 5.0, coupled with Inter-Tel.NET, NetSolutions and Inter-Tel software applications and hardware, the company had finally developed the ability to answer a company's complete communications needs.

By the end of the year, Inter-Tel posted record financial numbers based on the strength of AXXESS. Sales for 1998 increased almost 23 percent, reaching $274.5 million. Income was also the best ever, increasing 54.6 percent from $14.7 million to $22.7 million.

The New AXXESS

Released early as an all-digital phone system in early 1994, the first versions of AXXESS were solid and reliable but didn't offer the whole menu of options that the system was designed for. By 1998, AXXESS software was able to offer businesses a broad array of software applications. AXXESS 5.0 had another major benefit as well: It virtually removed the size cap associated with the system.

"It gives us the ability to connect multiple independent AXXESS systems together so they operate like a single phone system," said Jeff Ford. "Before 5.0, the largest AXXESS system that we could install might have 300 telephones on it. This allows us to sell systems that have 2,000 or 3,000 phones."[5]

For the first time, Inter-Tel could truly compete in the large-scale PBX market, where the profit margins were much larger, with a superior phone system. With the Inter-Tel platform, a company with thousands of employees in different states could have only one phone number. Each employee would be given an extension number, and the incoming call would be automatically routed to that workstation, regardless of its location. From the outside, it was seamless.

The market acceptance of the new AXXESS software, with its networking capability, was strong. In the first six months, Inter-Tel sold 800 systems that included networking software.

In terms of compatibility, AXXESS 5.0 boasted another powerful new upgrade in the form of a new operating system. Inter-Tel's phone systems had run on the same proprietary operating system since 1983. As computer telephone integration (CTI) became a reality, however, it became necessary for Inter-Tel to network systems that would work seamlessly with thousands of desktop devices and computers. Inter-Tel decided to adapt by moving some AXXESS systems to Microsoft's popular Windows NT operating system, Ford said.

"Having a standard operating system like that brings a lot more to the table than we lose. Historically, if we go back and take a look at PBXs in the 1980s, a lot of PBXs had disks in them for storing data, and they had their own floppy drives. Those PBX companies had to

create their own disk operating systems. If you're using a standard platform like Windows NT, all of those features are available to you. You don't need to develop a driver to access a disk. The underlying operating system also brings other things, like access to networks, networking compatibility, messaging and different applications like that." [6]

Working with a Net

AXXESS provided another important piece of the puzzle through its relationship to Inter-Tel.NET. By 1999, it was apparent that Internet telephony had not taken off as many had expected. In 1998, Ross McAlpine said Inter-Tel had sold only about $6 million in Internet-related products. This lag actually helped Inter-Tel because it gave the company valuable time to invest in the technology that experts still predict will change communication. Throughout 1998, Inter-Tel had been actively adding partners to Inter-Tel.NET. Overseas, the Japanese partner was joined by 12 European cities by 1999. Another partner was deploying gateways in South America, and yet more were working in Southeast Asia.

"We've just recently started selling Internet telephony over the network," McAlpine said in early 1999 of the expanding network. "Up until now, it's primarily been development of the servers, development of the accounting software and putting the network together. But since we started selling, our revenues on the network are increasing at a very fast rate." [7]

As was happening with other emerging technologies, the quality of voice-over-the-Internet applications was improving rapidly. By 1999, the lag time had been significantly reduced and voice quality was somewhat better than a cellular phone's. Plus, the price savings were astounding. In the cities with hubs installed, Inter-Tel.NET offered its long-distance service for as little as 5 cents per minute. The network's international rates were almost 40 percent below the prices charged by traditional long-distance carriers.

Eventually, McAlpine said, voice would be considered just another piece of the data chain, and the per-minute system of billing would vanish.[8]

TMSI

Investment in the new technology didn't end with new partners on the network. In mid-1998, Inter-Tel completed its first technology-related acquisition when it bought Telecom Multimedia Systems, Inc., or TMSI. The company, with very little revenue but powerful and valuable technology, was purchased for $25 million. TMSI specialized in voice compression software for IP telephony application and routers. Previously, Inter-Tel had been buying this technology for its Internet servers and hubs from an outside vendor.

"TMSI had some of the core voice-over IP technology, like voice compression, packetization and also basic router functionality," Ford said. "With the TMSI acquisition, we got more cost-effective technology."

TMSI, and indeed all of Inter-Tel.NET, was one piece in the larger puzzle that Inter-Tel executives had begun assembling years ago when they predicted that the conventional data network and the voice network would someday merge. In 1999, company executives began planning for the next generation of AXXESS, an advanced platform that would allow whole phone systems to jump to the Internet or privately operated data networks.

In this event, Inter-Tel would completed its transformation. Much more than a phone equipment supplier, Inter-Tel could offer its customer the entire portfolio of communications needs. Customers could buy or lease CTI applications, receive their voice mails and route calls through Inter-Tel software and, finally, transmit the calls through Inter-Tel routers over private data networks or the Internet. And they would be able to do all of this at a fraction of the cost charged by conventional phone companies.

"This is how we differentiate ourselves from the competition," said Ross McAlpine.

"We sell service. We say, 'Mr. Customer, what's important to you is not that telephone, that piece of plastic on your desk with the buttons. Inter-Tel, through its services and software applications, provides your total communications, and that's what's important.' Our competitors that stayed with only equipment sales got themselves in trouble."[9]

Buying Power

All of these developments — the TMSI acquisition, the AXXESS platforms, the developing IP telephony — were integral parts of Inter-Tel's plan for the future. Yet as had happened before, the path would not always be smooth, due to Inter-Tel's willingness to gamble. Even as the TMSI acquisition closed, Mihaylo and his team of senior managers were working on much larger deals, whole-company acquisitions far beyond anything Inter-Tel had ever attempted before. Instead of buying only distribution or even technology, Inter-Tel was planning on using its financial health to purchase its largest competitors in its core businesses.

The first acquisition was unveiled in October 1999, when Inter-Tel announced it had agreed to buy the computer telephone division of Executone Information Systems, Inc.

The decision to purchase Executone was a logical one but not a new one. In the mid-1980s, at the height of its strength (while Inter-Tel was still a $50 million company), Executone boasted wholesale sales of more than $200 million. But as had happened to so many others in the industry, the years had not been kind to Executone. Its phone system business had greatly diminished even as Inter-Tel continued to grow and strengthen.

By the time the acquisition was announced, Executone was a three-division company. In addition to its telephone business, which was very similar to Inter-Tel's, it also ran an Internet lottery and had a healthcare division. Executone's board had decided to divest the telephony and healthcare divisions and concentrate solely on the Internet lottery. At first glance, Inter-Tel seemed to be the perfect home for its telephony portion.

"In addition to expanding Inter-Tel's distribution base and market share, the acquisition will give Inter-Tel more extensive employee resources and an expanded customer base," Mihaylo said.[10] Moreover, Executone had a visible and well-known brand and did a sizable business in government contracts/national accounts, an area that Inter-Tel hadn't previously pursued.

Probably the biggest difference between the two companies was their distribution networks. Inter-Tel had always maintained an equal balance between direct dealers and distributors. Executone, however, divested its direct sales operation in 1996 and relied exclusively on dealer sales. Naturally, Inter-Tel hoped to keep most of these dealer agreements in place and begin moving AXXESS products into the Executone distribution channel, while also preparing a new product line known as the Eclipse. To keep Executone's loyal employee base intact, Inter-Tel announced plans to maintain Executone's facility in Milford, Connecticut.

Announced in October, the acquisition was scheduled to close in late December, allowing for two months of due diligence. During this time, Inter-Tel conducted interviews with senior management at Executone but, on advice of its lawyers, did not delve too deeply into the company's inner workings for fear of regulatory trouble. Bryan Dancer was one of the Executone managers who spoke with Inter-Tel representatives during the due diligence period.

As Inter-Tel prepared to close the deal, its own business continued to be strong. The company posted a record third quarter in 1999, then was honored by *Telecom Business* magazine as a Top 500 firm in the worldwide competitive telecommunications industry. "The companies selected to the *Telecom Business* Top 500 have positioned themselves on the cutting-edge of this rapidly changing industry," said *Telecom Business* publisher Marc Ostrofsky. "They are the movers, shakers and decision makers."[11]

At the same time, Inter-Tel was named one of the 200 best small companies in America by *Forbes* magazine. To qualify for that list, Inter-Tel had to boast a five-year annual growth rate of 10 percent and rank high in profitability and return on equity.

Cirilium and the Internet

In December, still waiting on the Executone deal to close, Inter-Tel announced another major strategic move: It had formed a joint venture with Hypercom Corporation, a publicly traded company on the New York Stock Exchange, to form Cirilium.

As one senior executive at Inter-Tel put it, Cirilium was basically "the combination of Inter-Tel and Hypercom technologies with some powerful advantages." Cirilium was chartered to sell hardware and software to the IP telephony service providers. Unlike Inter-Tel.NET, which sold long-distance service, Cirilium worked with carriers and large corporations that wanted to establish proprietary voice-over-the-Internet systems. Inter-Tel contributed its expertise with phone systems and CTI applications while Hypercom contributed carrier-class gateways, networking technology and electronic payment systems.

At the time of Cirilium's creation, the horizon seemed limitless: The system and equipment market for IP telephony was expected to reach billions of dollars in only a few years, and the quality of voice-over-the-Internet communication was steadily increasing. Tom Parise, the former president of Inter-Tel, soon announced he was coming out of his early retirement to act as CEO for Cirilium, thus adding a measure of stability for Inter-Tel, which was planning on a significant investment to make Cirilium work.

The Acquisition Closes

In late December and early January, just after this announcement, the Executone acquisition was finalized. All told, Inter-Tel had invested about $44.3 million in a major competitive brand, new offices in Connecticut staffed by about 400 employees and access to about 90 distributors.

The acquisition had an immediate and profound effect on Inter-Tel's market profile. According to market data from the Eastern Management Group, Inter-Tel became the largest provider of key telephone systems in the 40-plus-station key telephone market based on total systems and total stations or lines. It was even ahead of Nortel and Lucent Technologies. In the overall market for key telephones, Inter-Tel was second.

Strategically, Inter-Tel stuck with its plan. It would continue to distribute Executone's IDS, Eclipse, InfoStar, Medley and Sentinel products through the existing distributors, as well as add Inter-Tel products. While the company expected some distributors to cancel their agreements, management was generally confident that Inter-Tel could hold on to most of the dealer network. "We're delighted," Mihaylo told the business press.[12]

Unfortunately, serious problems bubbled up almost immediately. Looking back, Inter-Tel executives would see their mistake: For three critical months between announcing the acquisition and closing the deal, Inter-Tel had not been close enough to Executone's operations. In that time, production at Executone was curtailed, and the shelves were almost bare of inventory by the time Inter-Tel took over in January. "It was one of those assumptions," Dancer recalled. "I knew how bad things were in the manufacturing side, so I assumed that Inter-Tel understood how bad it was."[13]

Clearly, the lack of new product and ongoing problems with manufacturing upset a dealer network that was already unstable, and dealers began to cancel contracts in alarming numbers. Instead of losing a few, Inter-Tel suddenly faced the proposition of losing agreements with almost half of its new dealer network.

Inter-Tel, no stranger to crisis, approached this crossroad in typical fashion, turning to its management for strength. In the past, Inter-Tel had been able to count on tight and superior management and its dogged perseverance. This situation would be no different; company executives went to work in Connecticut to remedy the shortfall, and the board continued to support the acquisition. In the short run, there was little doubt the predicament would have a negative effect on earnings. Management intervention seemed like the best strategy for long-term gain.

Inter-Tel.NET

The problems at Executone were especially ill-timed for Inter-Tel because of a completely unrelated challenge. Inter-Tel.NET was continuing to expand exponentially, draining Inter-Tel of cash reserves with its voracious appetite for growth, especially in the Latin American market.

"Three years ago," said Jeff Ford in 2000, "we started Inter-Tel.NET to build a U.S. long-distance network, but it turned out because of the falling rates you see on daily commercials that in the domestic portion of the business there's just not a case for IP. However, there are still a lot of international locations where IP long distance is a significant cost reduction over traditional."[14]

As a signal of how important Inter-Tel expected this market to be, the company announced in March 2000 that McAlpine, who was president of Inter-Tel.NET, Inter-Tel Leasing and Inter-Tel NetSolutions, would assume responsibility for Inter-Tel.NET and Inter-Tel NetSolutions and that a new leader would take over the substantial leasing business. Later in the year, McAlpine also shed his leadership of Inter-Tel NetSolutions — a subsidiary that resold voice, video, data, and local and long-distance service — and devoted himself exclusively to growing Inter-Tel.NET.

To ease the financial burden of rapidly scaling up a business, Inter-Tel executives began to tentatively plan for an initial public offering of Inter-Tel.NET stock later in 2000 or early 2001. With the stock market booming for tech stocks, especially Internet stocks, and the quality of voice-over-the-Internet steadily improving, it seemed like the perfect time to take Inter-Tel.NET public. Plans were made for Norman Stout to move over to the newly public Inter-Tel.NET as CEO.

In April, however, at the same time board member Maury Esperseth announced his retirement, plans for the public offering were put on less stable ground. The Internet stock bubble — a major driver in the Nasdaq's upward climb — burst, beginning a long slide for technology stocks in general and Internet stocks specifically. With the stock market punishing this category, many companies postponed technology IPOs, and by the end of 2000, Inter-Tel was still waiting to take Inter-Tel.NET public.

This delay had more to do with market conditions than the long-term viability of Inter-Tel.NET. There seemed little doubt that Internet telephony would have a dramatic effect on the telephone market of the future — even if no one could predict exactly how. By late 2000, the cost of bandwidth was dropping steadily as new fiber-optic cables crossed the nation and the world. This decrease had the effect of lowering the cost of traditional local phone service, which likely contributed to the slower-than-expected growth of local Internet telephone service.

However, as Inter-Tel had predicted, moving long-distance IP business into foreign countries was an excellent idea. In May, Inter-Tel announced the acquisition of Intercomm Americas, Inc. (ICA), an IP telephony–based long-distance carrier with a network throughout Mexico. By the end of the year, Inter-Tel.NET was able to boast sales of about $22 million, a staggering growth rate of about 100 percent every quarter.

"Over the last year, ICA has built one of the strongest Internet telephony networks in this region," McAlpine said. "We are pleased that Inter-Tel.NET will be able to expand into Central and South America with the help of the Intercomm Americas staff."[15]

AXXESSing the Future

With the AXXESS product continuing to migrate toward an Internet platform (from version 5.1 forward, all AXXESS systems were IP compatible), the growth of IP telephony was of crucial importance to all of Inter-Tel. In this area, technology continued to move forward quickly. During 2000, Inter-Tel introduced a steady stream of upgrades and products that were aimed at turning AXXESS into an Internet PBX, offering advanced calling features to any size organization, be it a home office or a multinational corporation.

"There were two big highlights this year," said Ford in late 2000. "The biggest one is the integration of the InterPrise (IP) voice and data routers with AXXESS networking software. The AXXESS networking software is the software that allows the multiple switches, up to 63 of them, to operate as a single telephone system across different locations. This way, when you have multiple locations around the United States, you can get every one of the telephone systems to operate as if it were one large Inter-Tel phone system. That technology runs over IP networks, whether it's a corporate-wide-area network or whether it is the Internet."[16]

At the other end of the market, Inter-Tel's second big product release of the year was an IP key set card that allowed an individual IP key telephone to plug into an AXXESS system from a remote location. This had the potential of creating a truly viable home-office situation, with employees a seamless part of a company-wide network while still working from home.

These product introductions went smoothly, which was fortunate as the company was still working to correct the situation in Connecticut, fund Cirilium and invest heavily in Inter-Tel.NET's growth. Overall, Inter-Tel approached summer 2000 in a strange position. Its sales were excellent (a record $96.4 million in the first quarter alone), but overall the company posted a small loss of $1.5 million, its first in nearly 15 years.

Although this loss was small, it was a harbinger of things to come. Losses continued to mount throughout the spring as Inter-Tel struggled to get product flowing from Executone again. Finally, Inter-Tel's management decided to make a major move. In May, the company announced it was closing Executone's Milford, Connecticut, facility and moving all operations to Phoenix. "Executone is important to us," Mihaylo said, "and we value the associates who design, build and sell our Executone products. They need to be closer to Inter-Tel's headquarters to increase communication and to focus our commitment on the Executone brand."[17]

The Executone employees were offered transfers, and the facility in Connecticut was quickly shut down and relocated. Dancer, vice president of marketing, was one of the Executone employees who moved. According to senior executives at Inter-Tel, the move began to yield results immediately, at least partly by stanching the flow of money that was being consumed to increase inventory and rebuild Executone's distribution network. Inter-Tel soon announced that it would continue to sell Executone products to honor existing contracts and even introduce new branded products through the remaining Executone distribution network.

Financially, however, the worst was yet to come. In August, after again declaring record second quarter sales, Inter-Tel announced a net loss of $34.2 million during the second quarter of 2000, which included losses due to the investment in Cirilium, the troubles with

Executone and the ongoing and expensive efforts to ramp up Inter-Tel.NET. The largest and most painful portion of the loss was a $31.6 million net restructuring charge associated with the closure and write-off of assets connected with Executone. With the technology-stock market already going through a set of quirky cycles, sometimes even wandering into a bear market before vigorously rebounding, Inter-Tel's stock sagged on this news. The board of directors soon announced a plan to repurchase 2 million shares of common stock.

Only months later, Inter-Tel made another major move to address the ongoing losses at Cirilium. In September, the partners invited Paul Wallner, a senior vice president and the chief technology officer at Cirilium, to purchase a "significant stake in the company." Wallner was named CEO, replacing long-time Inter-Tel associate Tom Parise. Because of this move, Inter-Tel and Hypercom became minority owners and were no longer providing direct financing to Cirilium, thus preventing further losses.

By the end of the year, Inter-Tel managers looked back on an intense period and reflected on lessons they had learned from the Executone acquisition. "We learned to find out which people you're going to keep on the management team and to get them tied up," said Norman Stout, "and that it certainly is a lot easier to manage a larger facility locally than it is to manage two facilities split up by a large geographic territory."[18]

Moreover, said Mihaylo, Inter-Tel would be more careful during due diligence in the future and move faster to shut down a money-losing operation. "We shouldn't have waited six months to restructure Executone," he said that fall. "We should have restructured it on January first."[19]

However, Mihaylo said, the company was pleased with its record sales results during the third quarter:

"Our focus on offering total telephony solutions to our customers and recognition of the importance of voice and data convergence are the keys to our success. In view of the Executone restructuring in the second quarter, the write-off of the Cirilium investment in the third quarter and expected new product introductions, we currently expect good sales and earnings results in the fourth quarter of 2000 and for all of 2001." [20]

Another Major Buy

Inter-Tel management also refused to back away from its commitment to growth through acquisition. Although the Executone situation was a painful lesson in some ways, it was broadly seen as a growth opportunity and only a temporary setback. Moreover, there were other deals in the works.

On January 2, 2001, Inter-Tel management announced it was buying the remains of TIE/Communications, the once fearsome competitor that had boasted sales of more than $500 million. Since those days, however, TIE had become a greatly reduced company, through no fault of its employees or technology. TIE's problem was management.

Within a year of posting a half-billion dollars in revenue in 1984, TIE's sales had dropped dramatically, making the company vulnerable to a takeover by the Marmon Group, a private conglomerate of companies owned by the Pritzker family of Chicago. Marmon bought and operated TIE into the mid-1990s but, due to the ongoing industry challenges, decided to put TIE on the market. Inter-Tel jumped at the opportunity and put in a bid. Ultimately, however, Inter-Tel was outbid by Midco, a telco company based in Washington state. At the time, TIE was doing about $150 million in sales annually.

But TIE also fared poorly under Midco, and within two years the company was driven into Chapter 11 bankruptcy. Once again TIE was put on the market, and Inter-Tel prepared another offer for a company whose products and customer list were complementary to its own. And once again Inter-Tel lost the bidding war. In 1998, a communications company called Convergent paid about $70 million for TIE, including cash and assumption of liabilities.

But by late 2000, after two years of ownership, Convergent was also ready to throw in the towel and began soliciting offers for the remains of TIE/Communications. This time, Inter-Tel's offer was warmly received. Although the terms of the acquisition were not publicly disclosed, TIE registered about $70 million in annual sales by the time Inter-Tel bought it. More important than the revenue, however, was TIE's base of 32,000 customers and its cadre of seasoned employees.

"They've had real challenges, and candidly, those were no fault of the employees and associates," said Craig Rauchle in early 2001. "The business itself had been mismanaged by the people who had been supervising it, whether it was an investment group, a long-distance group, or Convergent and a system integration group. They've not had the keen focus Inter-Tel has."[21]

In fact, Inter-Tel's keen focus on its market and customers would be the greatest synergistic strength between the two companies. "What this transaction provides for Inter-Tel is really two things," Rauchle said.

"First, it's been Inter-Tel's philosophy from the beginning that it's very important for us to have direct contact with the end user. That relationship is important to us, and we believe that the more direct contact we have with our product through to the end

user, the better equipped we're going to be to deal with any changes.

"The second part is the quality piece. We have found that TIE has some very long-term quality people who we believe will be a tremendous asset for us. We expect to hire more than 200 quality people in technical services, sales disciplines and middle management areas. These are people who know the industry, and we believe these are people who will embrace our product and our commitment to the industry. They'll embrace our product direction and our philosophy."[22]

Even with the misstep at Executone, there was no denying how profoundly these acquisitions would change Inter-Tel. The company had grown into the undisputed leader in its market of 40- to 250-line business phone systems while watching much larger companies become crippled by competitive pressure. For example, Avaya — the equipment business that Lucent had spun off after itself being spun off from AT&T — continued to experience difficulties. In 2000, Avaya, an $8 billion corporation, announced it was selling its direct sales operation to Exp@nets, a division of Northwest Utilities.

Inter-Tel, operating from a balance of dealers and direct sales offices, had nearly 30 percent of the market and boasted record sales of over $400 million for 2000. The rest of the market, including Avaya's $300 million portion, was divided among a mishmash of companies all struggling for stability.

The Birthday Card Drill

Rauchle's observation that Inter-Tel's competitors were struggling to find their identities served to underscore one of Inter-Tel's most potent competitive weapons. In its 30 years of service, Inter-Tel had never strayed from its core business of small and mid-size phone systems. While other companies had bought, divested and diversified, Inter-Tel had steadily improved its offerings, gotten closer to its customers and stayed focused on its one segment of the much larger communications market. Even as the company branched out with Inter-Tel.NET, for instance, its main business remained the same, and Inter-Tel was increasingly watched in the media as a technology leader that helped define the future of business communications.

"The next generations of the AXXESS product will take on more of the form and function of a server," predicted Rauchle, Inter-Tel executive vice president and co-CEO in 2001.

"We expect that the 6.0 and 7.0 versions will move towards an application service provider (ASP) model in which the common equipment and applications run in server farms operated by Inter-Tel. We would bring those resources out to the end users through high-speed digital lines so the users wouldn't have the onus of having to maintain and update hardware and software."[23]

Inter-Tel's focus and its evolution into the leader of its market found their inspiration in Steve Mihaylo. Yet Mihaylo had always resisted the term "visionary," although it is the term heard most often when colleagues and friends are asked to describe him. The growth of Inter-Tel has mirrored the growth of the man who created it. From a young twenty-something on the road 80 hours a week selling an ugly phone, to a CEO running a company of nearly 2,000 employees, Mihaylo has surmounted the challenges of his career.

When Tina Sargent, his secretary who had quit Inter-Tel in 1988 to get married, returned in 1995, she was amazed at the difference she saw in her former boss. When she returned to the company, this time as executive assistant to Mihaylo, she had his complete confidence and eventually assumed the leadership of investor relations. "When I came back, he was a kinder and gentler Steve Mihaylo," she said. "Trust and loyalty are very important to him. It's really exciting for me when we're out on road shows and talking to investors and shareholders. It's a really good feeling to hear these people say to Steve, 'You know, you have done something at Inter-Tel that no one else has done.' It really makes me proud to work for someone like that, and he's very humble when he hears that. He acts like it's not a big deal."[24]

Despite the company's growth, Mihaylo is still able to stay close to the company and the people who work for him. In fact, he still composes and sends personal birthday cards to every employee of Inter-Tel in a time-consuming task Sargent refers to as the "birthday card drill."

"I present him with a stack of at least 150 a month, and he sits down, drags out these birthday cards and puts a personal note in every birthday card. We've had a lot of people say, 'Oh, Steve, I know that Tina just signs these cards, and we both say, 'No way.' I've asked him repeatedly to let me sign the cards, but he always says, 'No, absolutely not.'"[25]

Birthday cards are not the only challenge the growing company deals with. As Inter-Tel grew and purchased its largest competitors, it was confronted with the same issues that many much larger companies deal with regularly — how to stay innovative, yet grow; how to control the culture across a multinational corporation with thousands of employees; how to keep the company's spirit intact when circumstances turn against it. Inter-Tel had adjusted admirably to all of these challenges while flourishing in an industry that crushed thousands of others. The Inter-Tel culture kept the company together through close relationships that formed the foundation of the company's success. The company's cooperative spirit, constant quality improvement processes and ability to communicate with itself had created an organization that functioned smoothly and efficiently — or, as Mihaylo said, it's "like magic."

And, at least for the time being, Inter-Tel is safe from losing the vision of its founder and driving force. Although by 2001 he could have retired comfortably and relied on loyal employees like Craig Rauchle and Norman Stout to take over, Steve Mihaylo frequently says he won't leave his company before it reaches $1 billion in sales — which most people agree is not that far away.[26] Until then, his objective remains unchanged:

> *"I'd like to say that I was this guy who had a great vision of the future. But the only thing I can say that I really wanted, and I still want, is to build a big company, and it's still not nearly as big as I would like it to be. Our grasp has usually equaled or exceeded our reach. We realistically set our goals, and we've always been able to reach them."*[27]

NOTES TO SOURCES

Chapter One

1. Steve Mihaylo, interviewed by the author, February 7, 1997. Transcript, p. 83.
2. Bartlett, John and Justin Kaplan, *Bartlett's Familiar Quotations* (New York: Little Brown and Company, 1992), p. 741.
3. Steve Mihaylo, interviewed by Jon VanZile, June 10, 1998. Transcript, p. 21
4. Frank Lewis, interviewed by Ken Hartsoe, August 13, 1997. Transcript, p. 1.
5. Ibid., p. 3.
6. Steve Mihaylo, interviewed by the author, February 7, 1997. Transcript, pp. 50-51.
7. Frank Lewis, interviewed by Ken Hartsoe, August 13, 1997. Transcript, p. 4.
8. Campbell, Don G., "Court edict spurs competition for Ma Bell from new direction," *The Arizona Republic* (Nov. 13, 1971).
9. "Into a new age of technology," *History Time Line* (Sept. 2, 1997).
10. Stevens, William, "Phone Users Cite Service Decline," *The New York Times* (Jan. 22, 1969): 53:4.
11. Federal Communications Commission Reports, Docket No. 16942 (June 26, 1968): p. 1.
12. Conway Chester, interviewed by Ken Hartsoe, October 16, 1997. Transcript, p. 5.
13. Federal Communications Commission Reports, Docket No. 16942 (June 26, 1968): p. 1.
14. Steve Mihaylo, interviewed by the author, February 7, 1997. Transcript, p. 43.
15. Bird, David, "Phone Rates Are Linked to Monopoly Protection," *The New York Times* (August, 26, 1969): 35:2.

Chapter Two

1. Brooks, John, *Telephone — The First One Hundred Years* (New York: Harper & Row Publishers), p. 36.
2. Kraus, Constantine Raymond and Duerig, Alfred W., *The Rape of Ma Bell* (Secaucus, NJ: Lyle Stuart Inc., 1988), p. 21.
3. Boettinger, H.M., *The Telephone Book* (Croton- On-Hudson, NY: Riverwood Publishers), pp. 32, 30.
4. *Encyclopeadia Britannica*, Volume 28, 15th edition (Chicago: Enclopaedia Britannica, Inc., 1997), p. 473.
5. Boettinger, pp. 36, 38.
6. Brooks, p. 36.
7. Moncel, Count Du, *The Telephone, the Microphone, and the Phonograph* (New York: Harper & Brothers Publishers, 1879), p. 33;

Fischer, Claude S., *America Calling: A Social History of the Telephone to 1940* (Berkeley, CA: University of California Press, 1992), p. 35; Casson, Herbert N., *The History of the Telephone* (Chicago, IL: A.C. McClurg & Company, 1910), p. 108.

8. Kraus, pp. 19-20; Boettinger, p. 58.
9. Brooks, pp. 41-46.
10. Boettinger, p. 63; Kraus, p. 21; Brooks, p. 46.
11. *Ibid.*
12. Kraus, p. 21; Boettinger, p. 77.
13. Brooks, p. 37; Fischer, p. 36.
14. Ibid.
15. Noll, A. Michael, *Introduction to Telephones and Telephone Systems* (Norwood, MA: Artech House, 1986), p. 7; Wright, Charles Allen, *Telephone Communication* (New York, NY: McGraw Hill Book Company, 1925), p. 4; Johnson, K.S., *Transmission Circuits for Telephone Communication* (New York, NY: D. Van Nostrand Company, Inc., 1927), p. 1.

Chapter Three

1. Fischer, pp. 38-42; Noll, p. 11; Kraus, p. 27; Wright, p. 7.
2. Brooks, pp. 104-108; Fischer, p. 39.
3. Fischer, pp. 43-46.
4. Boettinger, pp. 112-114.
5. Brooks, pp. 115, 122.
6. Wasserman, Neil H., *From Invention to Innovation* (Baltimore, MD: The John Hopkins University Press,

1985), p. 109; Fischer, p. 46; Boettinger, p. 166.
7. Weinbach, M. P., *Principles of Transmission in Telephony* (New York, NY: The Macmillan Company, 1924), p. 203.
8. Fischer, pp. 61, 63; Kraus, p. 30; Brooks, p. 119.
9. Goulden, Joseph C., *Monopoly* (New York, NY: G.P. Putnam's Sons, 1968), p. 72.
10. Fischer, pp. 53-62.
11. Temin, Peter, Galambos and Louis, The Fall of the Bell System (New York, NY: Cambridge University Press, 1987), p. 12; Crandall, Robert Ward and Flamm, Kenneth, ed., Changing the Rules (Washington D.C., The Brookings Institution, 1989), p. 19; Kraus, pp. 171-172; Keller, David and Neal, Paul, Stocker: His Life and Legacy (Athens, OH: Ohio University Press, 1991), p. 40.
12. Fischer, pp. 51-53; Auw, Albert von, Heritage and Destiny: Reflections on the Bell System in Transition (New York, NY: Praeger Publishers, 1983), p. 65; Henck, Fred W. and Strassburg, Bernard, A Slippery Slope: The Long Road to the Breakup of AT&T (New York, NY: Greenwood Press, 1988), pp. 2-3.
13. Keller, p. 173; Crandall, p. 23.
14. Henck and Strassburg, pp. 12, 21; Crandall and Flamm, p. 20; Goulden, p. 106; Tunstall, W. Brooke, Disconnecting Parties:

Managing the Bell System Break-up: An Inside View (New York, NY: McGraw-Hill Book Company, 1985), p. 4; Keller, pp. 73-74.

15. Kleinfeld, Sonny, *The Biggest Compesy on Earth: A Profile of AT&T* (New York, NY: Holt, Rinehart and Winston, 1981), p. 155; Henck, pp. 26-27.

16. Coll, Steve, The Deal of the Century (New York, NY: Antheneum, 1987), pp. 58-59; Crandall, p. 114; Tunstall, p. 7; Henck, p. 62; Kleinfeld, pp. 76, 83; Crandall, p. 76.

17. Tuttle v. AT&T, FCC Rulings, 1948.

18. Crandall, p. 88; Henck, pp. 33-34, 36-37; Temin, p. 43.

Chapter Four

1. Anne DeRitis, "Choosing One's Life Work," (May 24, 1960), p. 1.

2. Ann DeRitis, "My Autobiography," (June 7, 1960), p. 6.

3. Ibid.

4. Ibid.

5. Ibid.

6. Steve Mihaylo, interviewed by the author, February 7, 1997. Transcript, p. 17.

7. DeRitis, "My Autobiography," p. 9.

8. Steve Mihaylo, interviewed by the author, February 7, 1997. Transcript, p. 12.

9. Matthew Mihaylo, interviewed by Ken Hartsoe, March 24, 1997. Transcript, pp. 3-4.

10. Davis, Adelle, Let's Have Healthy Children (New York,

NY: New American Library), p. 139.

11. DeRitis, "My Autogiography," p. 12.

12. Steve Mihaylo, interviewed by the author, February 7, 1997. Transcript, p. 13.

13. John "Happy Miles" Mihaylo, interviewed by Jon VanZile, January 26, 1998. Transcript, p. 10.

14. Andy Mihaylo, interviewed by Ken Hartsoe, April 22, 1997. Transcript, p. 9.

15. DeRitis, "My Autobiography," p. 12.

16. Andy Mihaylo, interviewed by Ken Hartsoe, March 22, 1997. Transcript, p. 4.

17. Steve Mihaylo, interviewed by Ken Hartsoe, March 6, 1997. Transcript, p. 1.

18. Andy Mihaylo, interviewed by Ken Hartsoe, March 22, 1997. Transcript, p. 11.

19. Ibid.

20. Steve Mihaylo, interviewed by Ken Hartsoe, March 6, 1997. Transcript, p. 20.

21. Steve Mihaylo, interviewed by the author, February 7, 1997. Transcript, p. 22.

22. Andy Mihaylo, interviewed by Ken Hartsoe, April 22, 1997. Transcript, pp. 10-11.

23. Steve Mihaylo, interviewed by the author, February 7, 1997. Transcript, p. 23.

24. Steve Mihaylo, interviewed by Ken Hartsoe, May 6, 1997. Transcript, pp. 37-38.

25. Ibid.

26. Ibid.

27. Steve Mihaylo, interviewed by the author, February 7, 1997. Transcript, p. 30.

28. Steve Mihaylo, interviewed by Ken Hartsoe, May 6, 1997. Transcript, pp. 33-34.
29. Chuck Mihaylo, interviewed by Ken Hartsoe, May 6, 1997. Transcript, p. 2.
30. Steve Mihaylo, interviewed by the author, February 7, 1997. Transcript, p. 37.
31. Conway Chester, interviewed by Ken Hartsoe, October 16, 1997. Transcript, p. 2.
32. Steve Mihaylo, interviewed by Ken Hartsoe, May 6, 1997. Transcript, p. 36.
33. Craig Dorsey, interviewed by Jon VanZile, March 2, 1998. Transcript, p. 4.
34. Matthew Mihaylo, interviewed by Ken Hartsoe, March 24, 1997. Transcript, pp. 10-11.

Chapter Five

1. Steve Mihaylo, interviewed by Ken Hartsoe, May 6, 1997. Transcript, p. 15.
2. Ibid.
3. Phoenix Chamber of Commerce, "The commercial-industrial climate in Phoenix, Arizona: Supporting the need and bid for a U.S. customs office," May 1970.
4. Luckingham, Bradford, *Phoenix: The History of a Southwestern Metropolis* (Tucson, AZ: University of Arizona Press, 1989), pp. 177, 189.
5. Ibid.
6. "Phoenix: One hundred years young, 1870-1970," Arizona Highways (April 1970): 16.
7. Johnson, G. Wesley, Jr., *Phoenix: Valley of the Sun* (Tulsa, OK: Continental Heritage Publishing, 1982), p. 164.
8. "Phoenix: the blemishes in boomtown," *Business Week* (November 15, 1969): pp. 144-150.
9. Luckingham, p. 210.
10. Steve Mihaylo, interviewed by the author, February 7, 1997. Transcript, p. 44.
11. Ibid.
12. Bill Bosse, interviewed by Ken Hartsoe, August 5, 1997. Transcript, p. 3.
13. "Open Season on Telephones," *Business Week (February 7, 1970): 58-60.*
14. Bill Bosse, interviewed by Ken Hartsoe, August 5, 1997. Transcript, p. 3.
15. Ibid.
16. Steve Mihaylo, interviewed by Jon VanZile, June 10, 1998. Transcript, p. 54.
17. Conway Chester, interviewed by Ken Hartsoe, October 16, 1997. Transcript, pp. 9-10.
18. Steve Mihaylo, interviewed by Ken Hartsoe, May 6, 1997. Transcript, p. 13.
19. "New Interconnect Entries Look to Burgeoning Market," *Electronic News* (February 14, 1972): 17:51.
20. Martin, Neil, "Dial-A-Breakthrough," Barron's (January 29, 1973), 53:3.
21. Ibid.
22. Bill Bosse, interviewed by Ken Hartsoe, August 5, 1997. Transcript, p. 10.
23. Steve Mihaylo, interviewed by Ken Hartsoe, May 6, 1997. Transcript, p. 15.

24. Steve Mihaylo, interviewed by the author, February 7, 1997. Transcript, p. 56.
25. Ibid.
26. Ibid.
27. Ibid.
28. Ibid.

Chapter Six

1. Steve Mihaylo, interviewed by the author, February 7, 1997. Transcript, p. 67.
2. Ibid., p. 65.
3. Ibid.
4. Craig Dorsey, interviewed by Jon VanZile, March 2, 1998. Transcript, pp. 7-8.
5. Steve Mihaylo, interviewed by Jon VanZile, May 15, 1998. Transcript, pp. 1-2.
6. Ibid.
7. Steve Mihaylo, interviewed by Jon VanZile, June 10, 1998. Transcript, pp. 2-3.
8. Tom Peiffer, interviewed by Ken Hartsoe, April 1, 1997. Transcript, p. 2.
9. Ibid., pp. 3-4.
10. Steve Mihaylo, interviewed by the author, February 7, 1997. Transcript, p. 66.
11. Tom Peiffer, interviewed by Ken Hartsoe, April 1, 1997. Transcript, p. 8.
12. Ibid., p. 7.
13. Ibid., p. 6.
14. Ray McCloud, interviewed by Jon VanZile, January 27, 1998. Transcript, p. 3.
15. Steve Mihaylo, interviewed by the author, February 7, 1997. Transcript, p. 67.
16. Tom Peiffer, interviewed by Ken Hartsoe, April 1, 1997. Transcript, p. 9.
17. Phil Moore, interviewed by Jon VanZile, March 3, 1998. Transcript, p. 3.
18. Zaffarano, Joan, "The New Telephones and All Their Smart Switches," Administrative Management, 36: 34-6.
19. Steve Sherman, interviewed by Jon VanZile, February 27, 1998. Transcript, p. 3.
20. Steve Mihaylo, interviewed by Jon VanZile, January 11, 1999. Transcript, p. 7.
21. Bill Nicewanger, interviewed by Jon VanZile, January 23, 1998. Transcript, p. 12.
22. Steve Sherman, interviewed by Jon VanZile, February 27, 1998. Transcript, p. 8.
23. Barry Wichansky, interviewed by Jon VanZile, February 9, 1998. Transcript, pp. 4-5.
24. Ibid.
25. Craig Rauchle, interviewed by Ken Hartsoe, April 9, 1997. Transcript, p. 2.
26. Ibid., p. 3.
27. Ibid., pp. 4-5.
28. Ibid., p. 4.
29. *Ibid.*
30. *Menshikov*, Stanislav, "How to Treat Stagflation," The New York Times (Jan. 5, 1975), Vol. III, 19:1.
31. Andy Mihaylo, interviewed by Ken Hartsoe, April 22, 1997. Transcript, p. 15.
32. Steve Mihaylo, interviewed by Jon VanZile, June 10, 1998. Transcript, pp. 6-8.
33. Cole, Joe, "Small firm bucks giant of industry," *Arizona Republic* (June 2, 1974): D-14.
34. Levine, Jon, "Inter-Tel; Phone maker capitalizes on ringing

market," Today's Business (May, 1981).

35. Ibid.

36. Brooks, John, *Telephone; the first hundred years* (New York, NY: Harper & Row Publishers), p. 315.

37. Stone, Alan, Wrong Number (New York, NY: Basic Books, Inc., Publishers), p. 288.

38. Koch, Walter, "Mountain Bell; Seventy-five years of growth and change," (Newcomen Society of the United States, New York, NY: 1986).

Chapter Seven

1. Tom Peiffer, interviewed by Ken Hartsoe, April 1, 1997. Transcript, p. 18.

2. Jackson, Tim, *Inside Intel* (New York, NY: Penguin Putnam Inc., 1996), p. 73.

3. Bersted, Howard, "Future Shock and the Telephone Industry- How Telcos are Coping," *Telephony* (May 31, 1976): p. 52.

4. Steve Mihaylo, interviewed by the author, February 2, 1997. Transcript, p. 68.

5. Tom Peiffer, interviewed by Ken Hartsoe, April 1, 1997. Transcript, p. 15.

6. Ibid.

7. Ibid.

8. Ibid.

9. Ibid.

10. Bill Ennist, interviewed by Ken Hartsoe, April 1, 1997. Transcript, p. 3.

11. Ibid.

12. Ibid.

13. Tom Peiffer, interviewed by Ken Hartsoe, April 1, 1997. Transcript, p. 18.

14. Ibid.

15. Ibid.

16. Bill Ennist, interviewed by Ken Hartsoe, April 1, 1997. Transcript, p. 5.

17. Ibid.

Chapter Eight

1. Steve Mihaylo, interviewed by Ken Hartsoe, May 6, 1997. Transcript, p. 17.

2. Briggs, Jean, "Shakeout in Progress," *Forbes* (July 18, 1983), pp. 93-96.

3. Baldwin, William, "For whom the bell tolls?" Forbes (September 14, 1981).

4. Tom Peiffer, interviewed by Ken Hartsoe, April 4, 1997. Transcript, p. 22.

5. Ibid.

6. "Phoenix-based Inter-Tel Inc. is a successful pioneer in the computerized telephone industry," Phoenix Business *Journal* (January 4, 1982): p. 12.

7. Ibid.

8. Ibid.

9. Ibid.

10. Steve Sherman, interviewed by Jon VanZile, February 27, *1998.* Transcript, p. 11.

11. Karl Eller, interviewed by Ken Hartsoe, April 1, 1997. Transcript, p. 6.

12. Levine, Jon, "Inter-Tel; Phone maker capitalizes on ringing market," Today's Business (May 1981).

13. Ibid.

14. Ibid.

15. Tom Parise, interviewed by the author, July 30, 1997. Transcript, pp. 3-4.

16. Ibid., p. 5.
17. Steve Sherman, interviewed by Jon VanZile, February 27, 1998. *Transcript*, p. 17.
18. Bill Ennist, interviewed by Ken Hartsoe, April 1, 1997. Transcript, p. 8.
19. Gerhardt Klaiber, interviewed by Ken Hartsoe, April 1, 1997. Transcript, p. 1.
20. Ibid., p. 2.
21. Terry Buffard, interviewed by Jon VanZile, March 3, 1998. Transcript, p. 3.
22. Steve Mihaylo, interviewed by Ken Hartsoe, March 6, 1997. Transcript, p. 18.
23. Steve Sherman, interviewed by Jon VanZile, February 27, 1998. Transcript, p. 21.
24. Karl Eller, interviewed by Ken Hartsoe, April 1, 1997. Transcript, p. 5.
25. Gerhardt Klaiber, interviewed by Ken Hartsoe, April 1, 1997. Transcript, p. 3.
26. Ed Terminy, interviewed by Ken Hartsoe, August 13, 1997. Transcript, pp. 16-17.
27. Jim Chumney, interviewed by Ken Hartsoe, April 1, 1997. Transcript, pp. 4-5.
28. Steve Mihaylo, interviewed by Jon VanZile, January 11, 1999. Transcript, pp. 15-16.
29. Steve Mihaylo, interviewed by the author, February 7, 1997. Transcript, p. 72.
30. Richard Long, interviewed by Jon VanZile, February 23, 1998. Transcript, pp. 3-4.
31. Ibid., p. 6.
32. Steve Sherman, interviewed by Jon VanZile, February 27, 1998. Transcript, pp. 18-19.
33. Ibid., p. 22.
34. Ibid., pp. 26-27.
35. Richard Long, interviewed by Jon VanZile, February 23, 1998. Transcript, p. 6.
36. Ibid., p. 6.

Chapter Nine

1. David Pheanis, interviewed by Ken Hartsoe, August 13, 1997. Transcript, p. 12.
2. Steve Mihaylo, interviewed by Jon VanZile, May 15, 1998. Transcript, p. 3.
3. Robert Craft, interviewed by Jon VanZile, April 28, 1998. Transcript, p. 5.
4. Tina Sargent, interviewed by Jon VanZile, May 11, 1998. Transcript, p. 9.
5. Maurice Esperseth, interviewed by Ken Hartsoe, April 2, 1997. Transcript, pp. 8-9.
6. Ibid., p. 7.
7. David Pheanis, interviewed by Ken Hartsoe, August 13, 1997. Transcript, p. 2.
8. Ibid., p. 6.
9. Ibid., p. 5.
10. Ibid., p. 12.
11. Pheanis, David, "Galaxy: Review of a software project," Phoenix Conference on Computers and Communications, Proceedings, (Phoenix, AZ: April 1986).
12. Skip Welch, interviewed by Ken Hartsoe, April 2, 1997. Transcript, pp. 5-6.
13. Jeff Ford, interviewed by Jon VanZile, October 29, 1997. Transcript, p. 2.
14. Maurice Esperseth, interviewed by Ken Hartsoe, April 2, 1997. Transcript, p. 4.

15. Tom Parise, interviewed by the author, July 30, 1997. Transcript, pp. 10-11.
16. Ralph Marsh, interviewed by Jon VanZile, November 7, 1997. Transcript, p. 4.
17. Briggs, Jean, "Telecommunications," *Fortune* (January 3, 1983): p. 213.
18. Hemphill, *Russ,* "Inter-Tel files $100 million lawsuit against Taiko Ltd.," The Phoenix Gazette (June 23, 1986).

Chapter Ten

1. Briggs, Jean, "Shakeout in Progress," *Forbes* (July 18, 1983).
2. Tunstall, W. Brooke, *Disconnecting Parties* (New York, NY: McGraw-Hill, Inc., 1985), p. 3.
3. Coll, Steve, *The Deal of the Century: The Breakup of AT&T* (New York, NY: Simon & Schuster Inc., 1986), p. 9.
4. Ibid., p. 43.
5. Tunstall, p. 13.
6. Coll, p. 44.
7. Ibid., p. 83.
8. Kirvan, Paul, "Divestiture: Its impact on end users," *Communications News* (January 1994): p. 11.
9. Tunstall, p. 11.
10. Ibid., p. 12.
11. Henck, Fred and Bernard Strassburg, A Slippery Slope: The Long Road to the Breakup of AT&T (Westport, CT: Greenwood Press Inc. 1988), pp. 203-204.
12. Strassburg, Bernard, "The Great Telephone Debate Drags On," Telephony (August 15, 1977), p. 22.
13. "The New New Telephone Industry," *Business Week* (February 13, 1978), pp. 68-78.
14. "Interconnect: The Big Market," *Purchasing* (February 10, 1976: 11.
15. "The New New Telephone Industry," *Business Week* (February 13, 1978): 68-78.
16. Coll, p. *110.*
17. Tunstall, p. 13.
18. Coll, p. 196.
19. Ibid., p. 78.
20. Ibid., p. 59.
21. Shoosan, Harry M., Disconnecting Bell: The Impact of the AT&T Divestiture (Elmsford, NY: Pergamon Press Inc., 1984).
22. Coll, p. 332.
23. Tunstall, W. Brooke, "Disconnecting Parties: Divestiture in retrospect — part I," *Telecommunications* (March 1992): p. 41.
24. Crandall, Robert, *After the Breakup* (New York, NY: Columbia University Press, 1991).
25. Briggs.

Chapter Eleven

1. Craig Rauchle, interviewed by Ken Hartsoe, April 9, 1997. Transcript, p. 25.
2. Maurice Esperseth, interviewed by Ken Hartsoe, April 2, 1997. Transcript, p. 7.
3. Craig Rauchle, interviewed by Ken Hartsoe, April 9, 1997. Transcript, p. 8.

4. David Pheanis, interviewed by Ken Hartsoe, August 13, 1997. Transcript, p. 23.
5. Ibid.
6. Pheanis, David, "Galaxy: Review of a software project," Phoenix Conference on Computers and Communications," Proceedings (Phoenix, AZ: April 1986).
7. Ray McCloud, interviewed by Jon VanZile, January 27, 1998. Transcript, p. 6.
8. Jim Chumney, interviewed by Ken Hartsoe, April 1, 1997. Transcript, p. 5.
9. Inter-Tel Annual Report, 1985.
10. Maurice Esperseth, interviewed by Ken Hartsoe, April 2, 1997. Transcript, p. 15.
11. Steve Mihaylo, interviewed by the author, November 3, 1997. Transcript, p. 28.
12. Crouch, Jean, "Valley companies form strategies in post-divestiture phone market," *Arizona Business Gazette* (September 1, 1986).
13. Steve Mihaylo, interviewed by Ken Hartsoe, May 6, 1997. Transcript, p. 20.
14. Ibid.
15. *Maurice Esperseth, interviewed by Ken Hartsoe, April 2, 1997. Transcript, p. 12.*
16. Craig Rauchle, interviewed by Ken Hartsoe, April 9, 1997. Transcript, p. 25.
17. Crouch, Jean, "Valley companies form strategies in post-divestiture phone market," *Arizona Business Gazette* (September 1, 1986).
18. "Inter-Tel finishes merger with Interconnect Corp.," *The*

Arizona Republic (October 25, 1987): E5.
19. John Gardner, interviewed by Jon VanZile, November 25, 1997. Transcript, p. 2.
20. Ibid.
21. Inter-Tel Annual Report, 1987.
22. Inter-Tel Annual Report, 1988.
23. "Inter-Tel's top executive asserts that stock has been undervalued," The Business Journal (November 21, 1988).
24. "Arizonans are optimistic on economy," *The Arizona Republic* (November 5, 1989): E1.
25. "Inter-Tel expanding overseas targets Japan, United Kingdom," *The Arizona Republic* (April 28, 1989): F7.
26. Inter-Tel Annual Report, 1989, Inter-Tel Annual Report, 1990.
27. Inter-Tel Annual Report, 1990.
28. Steve Mihaylo, interviewed by the author, February 7, 1997. Transcript, p. 74.
29. Inter-Tel Annual Report, 1989.
30. Tom Parise, interviewed by the author, July 30, 1997. Transcript, p. 15.
31. Jim Chumney, interviewed by Jon VanZile, April 1, 1997. Transcript, p. 9.
32. Tom Parise, interviewed by the author, July 30, 1997. Transcript, p. 13.
33. Ibid., pp. 15-16.
34. Ibid., p. 15.

Chapter Twelve

1. Jim Chumney, interviewed by Ken Hartsoe, April 1, 1997. Transcript, p. 13.

2. Luebke, Cathy, "Inter-Tel expands its business telecommunications systems," *The Business Journal* (December 23, 1991).

3. Maher, H.R., "Inter-Tel, Inc. - Company Report," Hancock Institutional Equity services (December 2, 1993).

4. Chuck Oakley, interviewed by Jon VanZile, October 29, 1997. Transcript, p. 11.

5. Ibid., p. 3.

6. Ibid., p. 4.

7. Maher.

8. Langham, A.G., "Inter-Tel - Company Report," Natwest Securities Corporation (February 18, 1994).

9. Steve Mihaylo, interviewed by Jon VanZile, February 11, 1999. Transcript, pp. 14-15.

10. Inter-Tel Annual Report, 1991.

11. Reilly, Bob, "Inter-Tel set to swap efforts over to U.S.," *Tempe Daily News* (May 1, 1992).

12. Laing, Jonathan, "Phoenix Descending; Is boomtown U.S.A. going bust?" Barron's (December 19, 1988): 8.

13. Bill Bosse, interviewed by Ken Hartsoe, August 5, 1997. Transcript, p. 19.

14. Fehr, Kerry, "Eller's selection to Inter-Tel board defended," *The Phoenix Gazette* (April 26, 1991).

15. Webster, Guy, "Inter-Tel reports loss, predicts gain," *The Arizona Republic* (April 26, 1991).

16. Steve Mihaylo, interviewed by Ken Hartsoe, May 5, 1997. Transcript, p. 20.

17. Tom Parise, interviewed by the author, July 30, 1997. Transcript, *p. 11.*

18. Langham.

19. Kurt Kneip, interviewed by the author, July 31, 1997. Transcript, p. 11.

20. Maher.

21. Langham.

22. Jeff Ford, interviewed by Jon VanZile, October 29, 1997. Transcript, pp. 4-5.

23. Barnes, Brady, "Move over, microprocessors," Telephone *Engineer & Management* (March 15, 1992).

24. Jim Chumney, interviewed by Ken Hartsoe, April 1, 1997. Transcript, p. 13.

25. Inter-Tel Annual Report, 1993.

26. Maher.

Chapter Thirteen

1. Steve Mihaylo, interviewed by the author, November 3, 1997. Transcript, p. 18.

2. Ray McCloud, interviewed by Jon VanZile, January 27, 1998. Transcript, pp. 17-18.

3. Steve Mihaylo, interviewed by the author, November 3, 1997. Transcript, p. 18.

4. Jeff Ford, interviewed by Jon VanZile, October 29, 1997. Transcript, pp. 10-11.

5. Thomas, K.E., "Inter-Tel, Incorporated - Company Report," *The Red Chip Review* (June 17, 1997).

6. Ross McAlpine, interviewed by Jon VanZile, January 7, 1999. Transcript, pp. 6-7.

7. Becklean, W.R., et al , "Inter-Tel, Inc. - Company Report,"

Hancock Institutional Equity Services, March 20, 1995.

8. Schneider, Paul, "Inter-Tel answering many calls telecom firm aiming for one-stop reputation," *Arizona Business Gazette* (May 4, 1995).

9. Craig Rauchle, interviewed by Ken Hartsoe, April 9, 1997. Transcript, p. 12.

10. Chuck Mihaylo, interviewed by Ken Hartsoe, May 6, 1997. Transcript, p. 12.

11. John O'Block, interviewed by the author, July 31, 1997. Transcript, p. 6.

12. Becklean.

13. Chuck Mihaylo, interviewed by Ken Hartsoe, May 6, 1997. Transcript, p. 14.

14. John Gardner, interviewed by Jon VanZile, November 25, 1997. Transcript, pp. 14-15.

15. Tom Parise, interviewed by the author, July 30, 1997. Transcript, pp. 18-19.

16. Craig Rauchle, interviewed by Ken Hartsoe, April 9, 1997. Transcript, p. 16.

17. Inter-Tel press release, INTL 94-3 (May 26, 1994).

18. Inter-Tel Annual Report, 1995.

19. Inter-Tel Annual Report, 1996.

20. Bill Nicewanger, interviewed by Jon VanZile, January 23, 1998. Transcript, pp. 3-4.

21. Buck, E.C., et al , "Inter-Tel Inc.–Company Report," Donaldson, Lufkin & Jenrette Securities (December 16, 1996).

22. Chuck Oakley, interviewed by Jon VanZile, October 29, 1997. Transcript, pp. 18-19.

23. Langham, A.G., "Inter-Tel - Company Report," Natwest Securities Corporation, February 18, 1994.

24. Buck, E.C., et al.

25. Ibid.

26. Dave Pheanis, interviewed by Ken Hartsoe, August, 13, 1997. Transcript, p. 17.

27. Laube, David, "Let the race begin," *Financial Executive* (September/October 1996): p. 27.

28. Telecommunications Act of 1996, 104th Congress, 110 Stat. 56.

29. Simons, John, "One-stop shopping in the telecom market; consumers are demanding bundled services," U.S. News & World Report (September 9, 1996): 42.

30. Ibid.

31. "Let the race begin," *Financial Executive* (September/October 1996): p. 27.

32. Steve Mihaylo, interviewed by Jon VanZile, January 11, 1999. Transcript, pp. 17-18.

Chapter Fourteen

1. Steve Mihaylo, interviewed by the author, November 3, 1997. Transcript, p. 5.

2. Steve Mihaylo, interviewed by Jon VanZile, May 15, 1998. Transcript, p. 3.

3. Hafner, Katie and Matthew Lyon, Where Wizards Stay up Late (New York, NY: Simon & Schuster, 1996), p. 77.

4. Hafner, pp. 56-57.

5. Ibid., pp. 62-63.

6. Ibid., pp. 60-61.

7. Kantrowitz, Barbara and Adam Rogers, "The birth of the Internet," *Newsweek* (August 8, 1994): p. 57.

8. Ibid., p. 56.

9. Fenton, Bruce C., "Death of the Internet," Popular Mechanics (January 1997): 41; Hafner, p. 227.

10. Miller, Michael J., "1995-1997: the on-line age," *PC Magazine* (March 25, 1997): p. 134.

11. Miller, p. 134.

12. Hauben, Michael and Ronda Hauben, Netizens: On the history and impact of Usenet and the Internet (Los Alamitos, CA: IEEE Computer Society Press), p. xiii; "The shape of nets to come," The Economist (July 1, 1995): S1; Statistics drawn from eMarketer website, www.emarketer.com: 1998.

13. Wetmore, John, "The Internet and its impact on people and society," *CMA - The Management Accounting Magazine* (November, 1997): 6; Statistics drawn from eMarketer website, www.emarketer.com: 1998.

14. Flanagan, Patrick, "Inexpensive long distance via the Internet?" *Telecommunications* (May 1995): p. 17.

15. Hafner, p. 232.

16. Flanagan, p. 17.

17. Meyers, Jason, "Market struggle plagues Internet voice products," Telephony (June 12, 1995): 16.

18. Steve Mihaylo, interviewed by the author, November 3, 1997. Transcript, p. 2.

19. Mark Hamblin, interviewed by Jon VanZile, November 21, 1997. Transcript, p. 4.

20. Jeff Ford, interviewed by Jon VanZile, October 29, 1997. Transcript, p. 15.

21. "Inter-Tel's good as gold gateway," *Computer Telephony* (December 1997).

22. "Inter-Tel calling shots for computer telephony," *The Business Journal* (January 30, 1998): p. 39.

23. Gwynne, Peter, "Internet telephony starts to make connections," *R&D* (November 1997): p. 24.

24. Mike Sargent, interviewed by Jon VanZile, October 28, 1997. Transcript, pp. 6-7.

25. Savitz, Eric, "'Net threat," *Barron's* (October 13, 1997): p. 37.

26. Fehr-Snyder, Kerry, "Investors discover Chandler, Ariz.-based Inter-Tel, drive up stock prices," Knight-Ridder/ Tribune Business News (September 10, 1997): p. 9.

27. Shonstrom, M.E., "Inter-Tel, Inc. - Company Report," Neidiger, Tucker, Bruner, Inc., September 15, 1997.

28. Inter-Tel press release (September 24, 1997), 97-11.

29. Goldblatt, Henry, "Your next phone call may be via the Net," Fortune (June 23, 1997), p. 139.

30. Steinberg, Steve, "Phone giants see future, and its Internet," Business First-Columbus (August 15, 1997): p. 21.

31. Fenton, Bruce, "Death of the Internet," *Popular Mechanics* (January 1997): 41.
32. Steve Mihaylo, interviewed by the author, November 3, 1997. Transcript, p. 5.
33. Savitz, Eric, "'Net threat," *Barron's* (October 13, 1997): p. 37.
34. Barbetta, Frank, "Regulation: it ain't over," *Business Communications Review* (September 1996): p. 51.

Chapter Fifteen

1. Steve Mihaylo, interviewed by the author, November 3, 1997. Transcript, pp. 10-11.
2. Norman Stout, interviewed by Jon VanZile, January 7, 1999. Transcript, p. 5.
3. Ibid., pp. 10-11.
4. Steve Mihaylo, interviewed by Jon VanZile, January 11, 1999. Transcript, p. 3.
5. Jeff Ford, interviewed by Jon VanZile, January 6, 1999. Transcript, pp. 3-4.
6. Jeff Ford, interviewed by Jon VanZile, October 29, 1997. Transcript, pp. 7-8.
7. Ross McAlpine, interviewed by Jon VanZile, January 7, 1999. Transcript, p. 10.
8. Ibid., p. 14.
9. Ibid., p. 9.
10. Steve Mihaylo, PR NewsWire, October 18, 1999.
11. "Telecom Business Magazine Names Inter-Tel as TOP 500 Firm in the Worldwide Competitive Telecom Industry," PR NewsWire, November 11, 1999.
12. "Inter-Tel Finalizes Acquisition of Executone Information Systems' Computer Telephony Division," PR NewsWire, January 4, 2000.
13. Bryan Dancer, interviewed by Jon VanZile, September 23, 2000. Transcript, p. 4.
14. Jeff Ford, interviewed by Jon VanZile, September 18, 2000. Transcript, p. 13.
15. "Inter-Tel.net Announces Acquisition of Intercomm Americas, IP Telephony Provider for Mexico and South America," PR NewsWire, May 9, 2000.
16. Jeff Ford, interviewed by Jon VanZile, September 18, 2000. Transcript, p. 10.
17. "Inter-Tel to Move Executone Milford, CT, Operations to Phoenix," BusinessWire, May 22, 2000.
18. Norman Stout, interviewed by Jon VanZile, August 30, 2000. Transcript, p. 8.
19. Steve Mihaylo, interviewed by Jon VanZile, August 25, 2000. Transcript, p. 6.
20. "Inter-Tel Announces 2000 Third Quarter Results," PR NewsWire, October 23, 2000.
21. Craig Rauchle, interviewed by Jon VanZile, January 17, 2001. Transcript, p. 4.
22. Craig Rauchle, interviewed by Jon VanZile, January 17, 2001. Transcript, pp. 6-7.
23. Craig Rauchle, interviewed by Jon VanZile, October

16, 2000. Transcript,
p. 6.

24. Tina Sargent, interviewed
by Jon VanZile, May 11,
1998. Transcript, pp. 29-30.

25. Ibid., pp. 34-35.

26. Steve Mihaylo, interviewed by
Ken Hartsoe, May 6, 1997.
Transcript, p. 23.

27. Steve Mihaylo, interviewed by
the author, November 3,
1997. Transcript, p. 41.

INDEX